T0121401

THE LIFE AND LEGACY

OF

"Allen Subdivision"

An African American Community
from the Early 1900s to 2015

DELORIS M. HARPOOL

authorHOUSE

AuthorHouse™
1663 Liberty Drive
Bloomington, IN 47403
www.authorhouse.com
Phone: 833-262-8899

© 2022 Deloris M. Harpool. All rights reserved.

No part of this book may be reproduced, stored in a retrieval system, or
transmitted by any means without the written permission of the author.

Published by AuthorHouse 11/08/2022

ISBN: 978-1-6655-7241-5 (sc)
ISBN: 978-1-6655-7240-8 (e)

Library of Congress Control Number: 2022918181

Print information available on the last page.

Any people depicted in stock imagery provided by Getty Images are models,
and such images are being used for illustrative purposes only.
Certain stock imagery © Getty Images.

This book is printed on acid-free paper.

Because of the dynamic nature of the Internet, any web addresses or links contained in
this book may have changed since publication and may no longer be valid. The views
expressed in this work are solely those of the author and do not necessarily reflect the views
of the publisher, and the publisher hereby disclaims any responsibility for them.

CONTENTS

DEDICATION

This narrative is dedicated to the highly esteemed Village Builders—the parents, grandparents, aunts, uncles, senior neighbors, older siblings, friends, and mentors of the community in Tallahassee, Florida, called Allen Subdivision. Although some of the Builders have made their spiritual transitions, the community remembers and honors them, as well as other Allen Subdivision Super Significant Seniors noted on pages 50 through 57. These seniors and their parents, in some cases, provided the loving, safe, Christian-based and encouraging environment necessary for a thriving, close-knit community. While facing incredible odds, they made it possible for the collective Allen family to maintain happiness, joy, peace, and hope for a future marked with strong men and women of noteworthy success in life. While providing for basic needs—food, shelter, and clothing—they led by example, teaching important lessons for endurance in the face of tremendous adversity. Allen is eternally grateful for the caring hearts, sacrifices, and influence of our Village Builders.

Lavern Washington receives 2015 reunion award for leadership/dedication
to Allen Subdivision. Image courtesy of Earl Washington.

Second, this document is dedicated to Mr. Lavern A. Washington, whose love for Allen Subdivision is unparalleled. He has been the core figure keeping the Allen Subdivision family together and its legacy alive. His loyalty to and love for the community have been evident via the sweat of his brow, the generous financial resources he has provided, and his sustained efforts to continue Allen Subdivision reunions as a way to keep the Allen family connected. It is with immense pleasure and appreciation that this author also dedicates this officially codified Allen story to the indisputable Allen champion, Lavern A. Washington.

FOREWORD

I am honored to have been asked to provide the foreword for this outstanding labor of love, which documents one of the founding communities in the City of Tallahassee.

For over eighty-five years, this small, historically African American neighborhood has been referred to by its residents as Allen Subdivision. It is little known to many residents outside of its boundaries, including city and county officials, like myself. Thanks to the work of a native daughter, Mrs. Deloris M. Harpool, this history has been researched, and many of us are learning that, at one time, this community was a flourishing, robust, significantly independent community of over two hundred close-knit families and over ninety bustling African American–owned businesses.

Mrs. Harpool provides great definition of the size and boundaries of Allen Subdivision to help us visualize where the events occurred. She takes the time to describe life for the adults and, most importantly, the children. She shares that it truly took a village to produce the fine caliber of citizens who emerged from Allen to be great leaders of today in their own right. Among the citizens described is the late honorable congresswoman Carrie Pittman Meek, who lived in this cherished community.

In the name of progress, this type of history is lost in many communities. I encourage each of us to follow her example and dig up, document, and educate others on the great legacy that has been passed on to us. We owe this and the preservation of our history to our future generations. Additional beneficiaries include the overarching city, state, and nation to which African Americans have added significant contributions and flavor.

Thank you, Deloris, for this great work, and I hope that more of us will catch this bug and get busy documenting our great legacy.

Dianne Williams-Cox
Commissioner
(Former Mayor Pro Tem
November 2020)

INTRODUCTION

My story is a freedom song from within my soul. It is a guide to
discovery, a vision of how even the worst pain and heartaches can be
channeled into human monuments, impenetrable and everlasting.
— Coretta Scott King

Allen Subdivision

The impact of urban redevelopment on African American communities has generated
increased interest across the United States. The process raises concerns related to
displacement of individuals from their initially affordable homes and long-term neighbors.
It also involves the loss of businesses and economic power in the communities being
affected by urban planning. Unfortunately, the process eradicates or significantly removes
remnants of lives that have added flavor to the broader community. Without efforts to
capture the essence of their homeplaces, African Americans lose volumes of rich history
and heritage. Such losses deprive a people, their offspring, and future generations of the
knowledge of their full identity, culture, heritage, and collective and individual worth.
These losses also tragically affect the entire, composite society.

The purpose of this document is to codify information about the African American
community in Tallahassee, Florida, known by its residents as Allen Subdivision. Also
known as Allen, this little-known site has existed for over ninety years in the south-
central segment of the city. Prior to redevelopment in this neighborhood, starting with
the 1986 erection of the M. S. Thomas Bridge and 2014 changes on Canal Street (FAMU
Way), there had been no known comprehensive, written account of the community.
In spite of racial discrimination and accompanying economic barriers, this community
found a way to survive, eventually becoming a thriving community full of life, love, and

highly supported enterprises. Its story and its beauty are worthy of review and historical preservation.

Essential as a backdrop to the Allen story, Jim Crow practices and laws collectively required the separation of citizens by race in the use of public facilities. During the early stages of development for the Allen community, these inhibitors dominated nearly all aspects of life for African Americans in Tallahassee and throughout the South. From the late 1800s, for at least seventy-five years, Blacks were not allowed to attend the same schools, theaters, or restaurants or sit at the same lunch counters and soda fountains as their White counterparts. Nor were they allowed to use the same hotels, swimming pools, parks, libraries, restrooms, or water fountains as Whites.

African Americans were required to sit in the rear section on buses and trains, separate from Whites. In the South, they were subjected to literacy tests, poll taxes in state and local elections, and other difficulties as they attempted voter registration. They also were denied equal access and equal opportunity in business and employment. In addition to wrongful and cruel treatment in the criminal justice system, Blacks were subjected to violence and attack by groups like the Ku Klux Klan if they violated the laws. In many cases, without any violation or just cause, Blacks were persecuted by White vigilante groups that often reigned without accountability or punishment.

Weathering the storm of discrimination, segregation, and economic challenges of the early 1900s and beyond was a noteworthy feat for early Allen residents. Before and after the passage of the Civil Rights Act of 1964 and the Voting Rights Act of 1965, which banned Jim Crow practices and expanded opportunities for African Americans, this community demonstrated tremendous resilience. Among the hallmarks of the residents of the community were their love for one another, their resolve to stick together, and their determination to ensure access to products and services within the local neighborhood and to ensure a brighter future for their children. The vibrancy of this treasured community was evidenced in its bustling businesses, spiritual beliefs and churches, enablement of folk ways, day-to-day activities, value of education, and interface with the neighboring Florida A&M University. With remarkable fortitude, this community made a sizable impact on the city's economy and on the production of contributing citizens in Tallahassee, the State of Florida, the United States, and abroad.

To ensure that city and county officials and others are aware of the significance of this cherished neighborhood is of grave import to Allen residents. This work promises to achieve that goal, in part. It illuminates details previously unknown yet valuable to the city, the state, and the greater American society, toward the preservation of the neighborhood's history. The material presented here is based upon multiple sources, including legal documents from the City of Tallahassee, official records filed at the Leon County Courthouse, and relevant literature. Records reviewed include property deeds, building permits, and city directories. Among other facts, this rendering takes a deep dive into Allen's lifestyle, early physical environment and living conditions, the initial owners of the developed tracts of land, the architectural descriptions of dwellings in the community, subsequent private homeowners, and documentation of the robust presence of African American–owned businesses.

The lack of specific dates in this document for certain events that occurred in the neighborhood is acknowledged as a limitation. However, there is significant concurrence and corroboration in the direct life experiences reported by over ninety informants. In addition to available documents reviewed, the accounts of individual informants were captured through written surveys, recorded oral histories, face-to-face conversations, telephone interviews, and the author's personal memoirs. Hopefully, this publication will enlighten, uplift, educate, and entertain readers while awakening treasured memories for Allen residents and individuals who grew up in similar communities.

Early Conditions: From Foot-Trodden
Paths to Paved Streets

In the early 1900s, before housing projects were fully developed, the landscape of the community historically known as Allen Subdivision featured open fields, hilly terrain, paths, and cow pastures. A wide variety of trees and vegetation added natural form, shade, and beauty, which would later become household perks in the area.

By 1944, foot-trodden routes, interlacing through the core of area fields, gave way to unpaved roads. Expanded housing developments brought a human element to the territory. For individuals who settled in the neighborhood, daily struggles to survive would ultimately forge close relationships among them, and they would bond with others who endured common conditions across the separately developed tracts of land in the vicinity.

Early residents of the community described conditions as vastly different from those experienced by residents who moved in after the late 1940s. "Things were very different in the 1920s and '30s," said Mattie Mobley, a long-term, previous resident of the community. At age 101, Mobley added, "There were just paths ... no electric lights in the homes or on the roads.... People had outhouses in their backyards for bathroom facilities."

Dorothy Carroll, wife of Fred Carroll Jr., owned two subdivisions in the area. She described what their tracts of land were like when they bought them, verifying that they "were just fields at the time, and the streets were paved later." She further discussed the green houses and block duplexes her family owned.

The green, wood-framed houses were built and then relocated to the first subdivision we owned. We continued to repaint all the houses in the same green color because it was more economical.… The block (duplex) houses were first built on Hudson Street. Half were rented to families and half were rented out to students.

When housing developments initially emerged in the area, no streets were paved. Open ditches, poor drainage, flooding, and muddy streets presented aggravating environmental hazards from Allen's birth through the mid-1950s. It wouldn't be until after the last platting in 1955 that a resolution was signed to complete the paving of all streets in the neighborhood.

Unpaved Hudson Street prior to December 1955 and front entrance to St. Michael and All Angels Episcopal Church (in background) before its change to Melvin Street. Image courtesy of Rosa Brown.

Lanell McCaskill, retired assistant principal and current doctoral student, shared reflections regarding environmental conditions during her childhood.

When we were growing up, we didn't complain about our environment. We didn't even think about it. We just played and had fun, sliding around on those muddy streets and wading in those rain-filled ditches. We had no idea how dangerous and substandard our streets and environment were, compared to those in more affluent neighborhoods.

Some of the streets in the neighborhood were not as complete or as long as they ultimately became after the 1940s. Mary Henry confirmed that the street previously known as Canal Street (now FAMU Way) was shorter before this period. She said, "It was just a path, and it didn't go all the way down to Railroad Avenue (Wahnish Way)." Other residents reported the many cow pastures that were originally in the area.

Documentation provided by the City of Tallahassee's Records Management Treasurer-Clerk's Office indicates that the Tallahassee City Commission began passing resolutions to improve segments of streets in the mid-1940s. One resolution states that, on June 25, 1946, the commission resolved to "grade, pave, install curbs or gutters, and install necessary storm sewers on Canal Street, from the east side of Railroad Avenue to the west side of Adams Street."

By the same order, the city manager was to "prepare plans and specifications" to improve a part of Boulevard Street (later renamed Martin Luther King Jr. Boulevard). The order specified that, from the south side of Canal Street to the north end of Florida A&M University's grounds, Boulevard Street was to be improved. This specific segment of a long street lies in the area considered to be Allen Subdivision.

Between 1953 and 1955, the city commission also passed resolutions to upgrade seven more of the eleven neighborhood cross streets in the same way. In commission records, the streets and specific segments to be improved during this period were identified as follows:

Harrison Street, from the west side of Adams Street to the east side of Boulevard Street (October 13, 1953);

South Bronough Street, from the north side of Palmer Avenue to the south side of Canal Street (December 22, 1953);

Melvin Street, from the north side of Palmer Avenue to the south side of Canal Street (February 9, 1954);

Van Buren Street, from the east side of Boulevard Street to the west side of Adams Street (June 28, 1955);

Hudson Street, from the north side of Palmer Avenue to the south side of Canal Street (December 13, 1955);

Jennings Street, from the east side of South Bronough to the west side of Adams Street (December 13, 1955);

and Pershing Street, from the east side of Boulevard to the west side of South Bronough (December 13, 1955).

Improvements for the final two streets flanking Allen Subdivision were ordered and incorporated in the above-listed resolutions between 1946 and 1955. These two streets were Palmer Avenue at Allen's south border and a segment of South Adams Street at Allen's east border.

How the Community Got Its Assumed Name

As of May 2015, and after extensive research, when and how the residential area called Allen Subdivision got its name could not be determined. Neither Leon County nor the City of Tallahassee has an officially recorded subdivision in south central Tallahassee by this name. Available documentation reveals that the geographic area, referred to by residents as one entity, does not exist as a singular, legal site. Particularly, it does not exist under the name of Allen Subdivision.

No person queried by personal interview, group discussion, or written survey for development of this publication could decisively state how the neighborhood got the name used to identify the community. Most fascinating of all, Allen Subdivision has been the name cherished and promulgated for over ninety years by residents living within the separate but physically connected and adjacent tracts of land. In addition, residents who adopted the community's unofficial title proudly refer to themselves as Allenites.

It is speculated that the name may have emulated the last name of C. K. and Della Allen, an enterprising couple who were among the early residential builders and developers in the area. Along with L. E. and Elizabeth McWilliams, the Allens platted, legally recorded, and identified College View as the name of the property they would develop on April 22, 1926.

Neither of the couples' last names was included on the title they assigned to their development. Their tract was near the former Reid Street, which later became Boulevard Street and was again renamed to Martin Luther King Jr. Boulevard. Theirs was only a segment of official, adjacent subdivisions and parcels later collectively considered by residents to be one, the Allen Subdivision.

It may be that the resident-assigned title is simply an altered form of "the Allens' subdivision." One might speculate that individuals from outside of the area and residents, themselves, without searching official court documents, assumed that all parcels in the immediate vicinity of the Allens' College View settlement belonged to the Allens.

It is possible that some residents and outsiders unwittingly initiated and promulgated the unofficial title as the official name of the composite community connected to College View. This, in part, would explain why previous researchers experienced difficulty in locating literature under the neighborhood's assumed title.

Another consideration is the very discrete boundaries that enclosed their socially close-knit community. These boundaries may have added to the residents' perception that they collectively lived in a singular subdivision. The boundaries are Florida A&M University's property, directly south and west of the area; the CSX Railroad tracks, directly north; and commercial establishments immediately east, on South Adams Street. These borders totally encircle and isolate the community from any other distinct residential tracts of land in the vicinity.

The Land Developers and Their Official Subdivisions

Available documentation reveals that the geographic area of 46.6 acres considered to be the Allen Subdivision actually consists of five legally assigned, adjacent tracts of land. Plus there are one major and three minor adjacent unplatted properties. The tracts, owners, and plat dates are as follows:

Palmer's Addition South Subdivision
Owner(s)/Developers: Robert B. Council and Ida Council
Platted February 20, 1908

Morrill Heights Subdivision
Owner(s)/Developers: J.T. Phillips and Elizabeth Phillips
Platted November 2, 1914

College View Subdivision
Owner(s)/Developers: C.K. Allen and Della Allen, L. E. McWilliams and
Elizabeth McWilliams
Platted April 22, 1926

Carroll's Subdivision
Owner(s)/Developers: Fred Carroll Sr. and Clara M. Carroll
Platted October 13, 1936

Carroll's South Subdivision
Owner(s)/Developers: Fred Carroll Sr. and Clara M. Carroll
Platted March 23, 1943

Taylor Development
Owner(s)/Developers: Robert B. Taylor and Elizabeth B. Taylor
Metes and Bounds Parcel (1946; Not Platted)
Official Record Book 862, Page 228
Official Record Book 76, Page 325

Family Dwellings

During the postwar years, when Americans in general began to prosper, African Americans throughout the United States continued to experience hard times. Looming Jim Crow laws and unfair hiring practices inhibited prosperous living for these families. Although they managed to survive, it was a struggle for African Americans with low-wage jobs to take care of their families. Their minimal earnings and limited transportation would require affordable housing in the vicinity of their workplaces.

The relocation of the State Normal and Industrial College for Colored Students in the 1890s stimulated housing developments in Tallahassee near the college. The fresh setting, south of the college's original Copeland Street site, would bring jobs likely to be filled by African Americans on Tallahassee's south side. The institution, later named Florida Agricultural and Mechanical College for Negroes (FAMC by 1909), grew exponentially by the 1920s. With the growth of the minority-run institution, more jobs became available for African Americans.

In addition, housing forecasters of the late 1800s may have influenced buyers to consider building in the vicinity of the college as a potential economic boon. Potential residents would be conveniently located near the state capitol building, downtown merchants, and other businesses to the north of housing developments in the area. Work within walking distance of these establishments, along with additional employment opportunities in commercial districts east of the new FAMC campus, would encourage residents to seek housing in the area, as well.

Responding to the need for suitable housing was easy and profitable for area developers. With great dispatch, builders were able to produce houses that fit their new residents' needs. Qualified architects were not required, and builders could use local materials and traditional construction techniques to erect homes typically built from pattern books or a builder's memory. Each dwelling was placed on a small lot, approximately one-quarter acre each, with shallow recess from the street. The newly built homes were simple, economical, functional, and comfortable.

Developers initially built homes in Allen very close to the northern and eastern edges of FAMC. The first settlement took root in 1908 when owners Robert B. and Ida Council platted the Palmers Addition South Subdivision near the corner of Boulevard Street and Canal Street (FAMU Way). Morrill Heights followed in 1914, directly across the street from and north of FAMC's campus. The College View Subdivision followed in 1926, carved out of Palmers Addition South. This change divided Palmers Addition into two parts directly north and east of FAMC's campus, along Boulevard Street, between Palmer Avenue and West Van Buren Street.

Richard and Eva Jefferson were believed to have been the first residents to build their home in Allen Subdivision. According to court records, the Jeffersons bought their lot from Robert B. and Ida Council on March 23, 1928, and later built their home at 1422 South Bronough Street in the Palmers Addition South Subdivision. By 1928, other official subdivisions had been platted and recorded in the composite area considered to be Allen Subdivision. The other preexisting subdivisions were Morrill Heights, platted in 1914, and College View, platted in 1926.

To assert that the Jeffersons' home was the first built in the greater Allen community would suggest that no other homes were built in the immediate area for twenty years, from 1908 when Palmers Addition South was platted to 1928 when the Jeffersons purchased their land. It would appear that other homes would have already been erected in two other, earlier segments of the greater Allen community before the Jeffersons' home was built in Palmers Addition South. Further research may be required to determine the sequence in which the Jeffersons' home and all other homes were built in the early segments of the composite Allen community.

By the mid-1940s, all homes built in Allen covered a range of common vernacular styles. They were built with composite-shingle or tin-metal roofs. Building permits filed with the City of Tallahassee show that plumbing was added to homes in the 1940s to the mid-1950s to accommodate attachments called water closets on the back porches of the earlier homes. These noninsulated wooden enclosures housed toilets only, without sinks or bathtubs.

By the early 2000s, a few more modern structures were visible in the area. Most of the original homes were still standing as of 2015, although they had undergone expansion or modification to accommodate updates and growing family or business needs. Between 1950 and 1959, the *Tallahassee Democrat* newspaper listed homeowners in Allen who were granted permits by the Tallahassee City Commission to make changes to their homes. Unfortunately, changes to the original homes throughout the community prevented the neighborhood from being cited as a National Historic Registry District.

As reported by the *Democrat*, some of the owners, their addresses, general permit types, and dates of publication of their permits are as follow:

- Arthur Mobley, 309 West Harrison Street, Residence Addition (*Democrat*, September 3, 1950)
- James Long, 218 Canal Street, Residential Alteration (*Democrat*, December 11, 1955)
- Joe Smith, 317 West Harrison Street, Residential Alteration (*Democrat*, December 11, 1955)
- John C. Allen, 317 West Harrison Street, Residential Addition (*Democrat*, March 15, 1959)

Many Allen residents currently live in homes that are more accommodating, spacious, comfortable and functional than those their parents could afford. Many lived in low quality homes with cramped quarters, but their parents would 'make do.' Some used rain buckets to catch water flowing inside from leaking, aging roofs. In some cases, three to four children slept side-by-side in one bed, often awaking to the question – "Who peed the bed?"

Listed below are brief architectural descriptions of the original dwellings in the community. Also listed are the addresses and legal names of the subdivisions where some of the original home styles existed by 1950 and remained visible as of 2015.

- **Craftsman Bungalow:** Easily constructed from a Sears, Roebuck and Co. mail-order-catalog plan, this style is simple in layout, height, and features. It is typically a cottage-like, single-story home with a low-pitched gable roof. In Virginia McAlester's description of the Craftsman style house, "Among the most distinctive features of the style are the junctions where the roof joins the wall, which are almost never boxed or enclosed. The roof has a wide eave overhang; along *horizontal* edges the actual rafter ends are exposed." In addition, "columns for supporting the porch roofs are a distinctive and variable detail." See the structure at 1451 Melvin Street in the Carroll South Subdivision.

Craftsman Bungalow. Image courtesy of Deloris Harpool

- **Minimal Traditional:** Without frills like porches or formal dining rooms, this house is modest in size and square (box-like) or rectangular in shape. It normally covers less than one thousand square feet of living space. As described by Virginia McAlester, identifying features of these homes are summarized as "low- or intermediate-pitched roof, more often gabled; small house, generally one-story in height; roof eaves usually have little or no overhang; double-hung windows...." See the structure at 1437 South Bronough Street in the Carroll South Subdivision.

Minimal Traditional. Image courtesy of Deloris Harpool

- **Minimal Traditional with Prairie Influences:** A variation of the minimal traditional home, this structure has ribbon-styled (side-by-side) windows as an added feature.

Minimal Traditional with Prairie Influence. Image courtesy of Deloris Harpool

(Note: Informant Irene Gilliam proudly reports that her father, Ike Gilliam Jr. was the talented builder of their family's home on Melvin Street.) See the structure at 1430 Melvin Street in the Carroll South Subdivision.

Home with screened porch built by Ike Gilliam Jr, captured on a snowy day in Tallahassee, Florida. Image courtesy of Irene Gilliam

- **Ranch:** Fashioned after the old California ranch house, this structure is a long, rectangular, shallow (one to two rooms deep) home with a shallow front porch and a large picture window on the front. It is a one-story structure spread wide across a lot, and it may be U- or L-shaped. McAlester presents this style as "broad one-story; usually built low to the ground; … commonly with moderate-to-wide roof over-hang; front entry usually located off-center and sheltered under main roof of house; garage typically attached to the main façade (faces front, side or rear)." A garage or carport is attached on one end of the house and sliding glass doors are featured on the rear. See the structure at 1525 South Bronough Street, Morrill Heights Subdivision.

Ranch. Image courtesy of Deloris Harpool

- **Shotgun:** Popular during the postwar years for their affordability, shotgun houses were simple, rectangular structures with rooms flowing from one to another without hallways. Because of its floor plan, as has been commonly expressed, a shot fired from the front of this style of house could travel to the back without obstruction. Author Virginia Savage McAlester describes these homes as "narrow gable-front dwellings one room wide that dominated many modest southern neighborhoods built from about 1880 to 1930." Among other "folk houses" described by McAlester, these houses were "particularly suited for narrow urban lots." Shotgun homes existed on Hudson, Melvin, South Bronough, South

Boulevard, Van Buren, Canal, Harrison, and Jennings Streets before some of them were demolished in the two Carroll's Subdivisions.

Shotgun house under restoration at 1313 Melvin Street. Image courtesy of Deloris Harpool

- **Two-Family Concrete Block Duplexes:** These were two-family, pastel-colored units that once existed in the Taylor Development at the intersection of Boulevard Street (MLK Boulevard) and West Van Buren Street. Under the same roof, each unit in this dual-family home was built in shotgun style with a shared divider wall separating the two families. Each unit featured a living room, which often doubled as a bedroom, a bedroom, and a kitchen with a small space for a table and chairs. The exterior entrance to the lavatory was from the back porch of each family's unit.

A few block duplexes built in similar exterior style were erected in Carroll's South Subdivision on Hudson and Melvin Streets. Similar to the dual-family homes in the Taylor Development, each family in these duplexes shared a common roof and a central divider wall. However, the Carroll's South Subdivision duplexes had a different interior floor plan, wherein the living room flowed into a kitchen with an exit door on the side of each family's unit. From the kitchen, there was a short hallway leading to an interior bathroom and two bedrooms at the rear of the unit. See the structure at 1436 Hudson Street in the Carroll's South Subdivision.

Block Duplex in Carroll's South Subdivision. Image courtesy of Deloris Harpool

As noted above, the earliest settlement in the Allen area appeared in 1908 in the Palmers Addition South Subdivision on Boulevard Street (MLK Boulevard). The last settlement in the area, the Taylor Development, appeared thirty-eight years later in 1946 on West Van Buren Street near its intersection with Boulevard Street. This site was just north of the canal that originally ran parallel to Canal Street (FAMU Way) between Railroad Avenue (later renamed Wahnish Way) and the west side of South Boulevard Street.

By 1960, the entire Allen Subdivision was fully occupied with at least 205 families. A map developed in 2014—with the help of staff of the Tallahassee Leon County Geographic Information Systems' Department of Development Support and Environmental Management (DSEM). It displays the 1960 location of each family by name, street address, block, legal subdivision or development and home ownership. The display is supported by information in the 1960 Florida Polk's Tallahassee City Directory.

Residences, Churches and Street Blocks in the

Families by Street, Address and Home Ownership (1960)

Produced by the Committee for the Preservation of History of the Community Called "Allen Subdivision"

S. Adams Street:
1510 - Pete Miller
1516 - Luke Thompson *
1518 - Malicious L. Lincoln *
1522 - Ora Young *
1526 - Minnie Spencer
1530 - Vacant
1540 - A. Ralph Hoffman *

S. Boulevard Street:
1304 - James Lewis
1306 - Emmett Jones
1308 - Inez D. Russell
1315 - Vacant
1315R - Vacant
1317 - Isaac Robinson *
1319 - Willie Hilliard
1323 - Phillip Dorsey *
1327 - Bessie B. Ford *
1329 - Vacant
1331 - Georgia P. Long *
1335 - Ernest Jones *
1339 - Robert W. Matthews *
1341 - Lula B. Young *
1401 - Charles E. Weaver *
1403 - Leroy F. Howard *
1413 - Eddie Williams
1415 - Melvin R. Kyler *
1417 - William Kornegay
1435 - Donald Bowles
1443 - Ewing T. Brooks *
1449 - Cecilia M. Mobley *
1503 - Zeora R. Hercey *
1504 - John R. E. Lee *
         A.D. Vinson
1535 - Joseph L. Tatum

S. Bronough Street:
1204 - Mamie E. Brazell *
1317 - Leamus A. Henry *
1318 - Ollie R. Brown *
1319 - John Henderson
1319 ½ - Garfield Stoney
1320 - Benjamin Long, Jr. *
1321 - Nancy H. Palmer
1321 ½ - King Solomon
1323 - McKinley Wilson *
1325 - Lena R. Beal
1334 - Ezekial Governor *
1337 - Abraham Washington
1338 - Arthur E. Johnson
1339 - Vacant
1342 - Ethel C. Williams *
1344 - Charles Young, Jr. *
1345 - Vacant
1349 - Lillian W. Hunter
1401 - Dallas R. Madison *
1413 - James C. Stretchings
1414 - Robert S. Sims *
         Birda M. Allen
1415 - Rosetta S. Yopp *
1416 - Vacant
1421 - Walter F. Lamb *
         Charles H. Wanza
1422 - Eva G. Jefferson

1423 - Willie S. Pittman, Jr. *
1431 - Eddie L. Smith *
1435 - George S. Green
1437 - William Jefferson, Sr. *
1441 - Earl H. Boyd *
1446 - Lee A. Royster
1447 - Carrie T. Pittman *
1452 - George W. Conoly *
1503 - Myrtle L. Ford *
1511 - Willie Floyd *
1525 - Moses G. Miles *
1527 - Alverta N. Morris
1529 - John W. Boardley

Canal Street:
114 - Ary R. Brown *
118 - Joseph Davis
121 - Gideon Clack *
123 - Gethsemane Church
126 - Phillip Young *
130 - William Lawrence *
134 - John Paramore *
216 - Estelle Washington
217 - Vacant
218 - James Long *
219 - J.H. Russell
219 ½ - Vacant
220 - William Jones
222 - Stafford Evans *
228 - Vacant

W. Harrison Street:
108 - Edward H. DeBose, Jr.
111 - Everett Flemming *
120 - Malissie F. Brazil *
206 - Alton L. Smith
305 - James E. Williams *
309 - Arthor L. Mobley *
313 - Willie C. Askew
315 - Vacant
317 - Corine G. Smith *

Hudson Street:
1306 - Lionel Ferguson
1310 - Namon Mills, Sr. *
1312 - Reddick Gibbons
1314 - Willie Brown
1316 - John C. Homer
1317 - Sally L. Williams
1318 - Floyd Brown
1319 - Henry L. Allison
1320 - Samuel Pittman
1321 - Arthur W. Seay
1323 - Jesse L. Mitchell
1402 - St. Michaels Church
1412 - Soloman E. Fields
1414 - Eddie L. Thomas
1418 - Joseph Rosier *
1428 - Elijah Pittman
1434 - Samuel J. Warren
1436 - Samuel A. Mayo
1438 - James R. Gibbons
1440 - Leroy Williams
1442 - Anne L. Corker
1444 - Thelma R. Sheppard

1445 - Arthur W. Carter
1446 - James W. Laing
1447 - Robert L. Anders
1148 - D.Q. Bassa
1449 - J. Tyrone Ferguson
1451 - Vacant
1511 - Vacant
1512 - Lula J. Brooks *
1513 - Tom Colson, Jr.
1514 - Minerva W. Holmes

W. Jennings Street:
115 - Simon J. Young *
119 - Joseph Bines *
123 - Judge B. Kendrick *
127 - Johnny Brown *
127 ½ - Hubert Brown *
211 - James Williams *

Melvin Street:
1301 - Dora M. Jones *
1302 - Alexander Henry *
1303 - Willie R. Long *
1308 - Eunice McCray *
1309/11- Ordray J. Washington *
1312 - Melvin Beal *
1313 - Arthur Givens
1314 - John Beal *
1315 - Shelley Gavin *
1317 - Virginia N. Shorter
1318 - Nancy Weaver
1320 - Leroy Brown
1322 - Martha B. Governor *
1326 - Vacant
1404 - Clarence Golden
1406 - Prince Hinson, Jr.
1407 - St. Michaels Annex
1409 - Edward L. Williams
1411 - Levi L. Moss
1413 - David A. Collins
1415 - Dorothy Snow
1419 - Corine H. Watts *
1421 - Mary T. Griffin
1428 - Ada N. Harley *
1430 - Ike Gilliam, Jr. *
1431 - Mary L. Hudnell *
1435 - Willie C. Smith *
1438 - Edna J. Anderson *
1439 - Rosetta E. Edwards *
1443 - Clyde L. Young *
1445 - Charles Daniels
1451 - William M. Burns
1507 - John Steele *
1511 - China B. Larkins *
1517 - Arthur Holt *
1518 - Nero Pender *
1522 - Leroy Beasley

W. Palmer Avenue:
104 - Fred Williams
108 - Charlie E. Jenkins
110 - Louise C. Fields
112 - Charles J. Stanley, Jr. *
114 - Kathryn M. Williams
124 - Albert R. Crump *

202 - Parker Hollis *
204 - Birdie L. Jones *

W. Pershing Street:
302 - Susie McLendon *
304 - Mary A. Larkins *
313 - Mathew H. Estaras *
319 - Allen P. Turner *
         Clarice J. Young

W. Van Buren Street:
107 - Vacant
211 - Roscoe D. Long *
215 - Jesse Ware *
219 - Lila M. Clack
223 - Robert L. Martin
227 - Richard Ford *
300a - Lee E. Triplett
300b - Emmette Ford
302 - Mamie L. Williams
304 - Vacant
307 - Lillie Smith
311 - Adolphus D. Williams *
315 - Joseph Nathen
319 - Johnny Herndon
323 - Harold L. Clack
400 - Elbert L. Humphrey
401 - Willie L. Allen
402 - Edward Pennie
403 - Wilmer Ferrell
405 - David Hatcher
406 - Clinton Russ
407 - Ellis Staten
408 - Willie J. Gatlin
409 - Daniel Ziegler, Jr.
410 - Alma J. Jenkins
411 - Jim Staten
412 - Ned Sanders
414 - Daisy B. Dewberry
415 - Dan Parrish
416 - Arthur L. Kimble
417 - Pearlie M. Staten
418 - Freddie Dorsey
419 - Willie Williams
420 - Alexina Kelly
421 - Mary Jones
422 - Iradella O. Watts
423 - Timothy L. Collier
424 - Sarah D. Way
425 - Arlene M. Randolph
426 - Emma D. Lockett
427 - Melvin Bacon
428 - John Davis
429 - Washington Woodall

* Home Owner (92)

Source: Florida Polk's Tallahassee City Directory, R.L. Polk & Company, Publishers, 1960

Area of Tallahassee, Florida Called "Allen Subdivision"

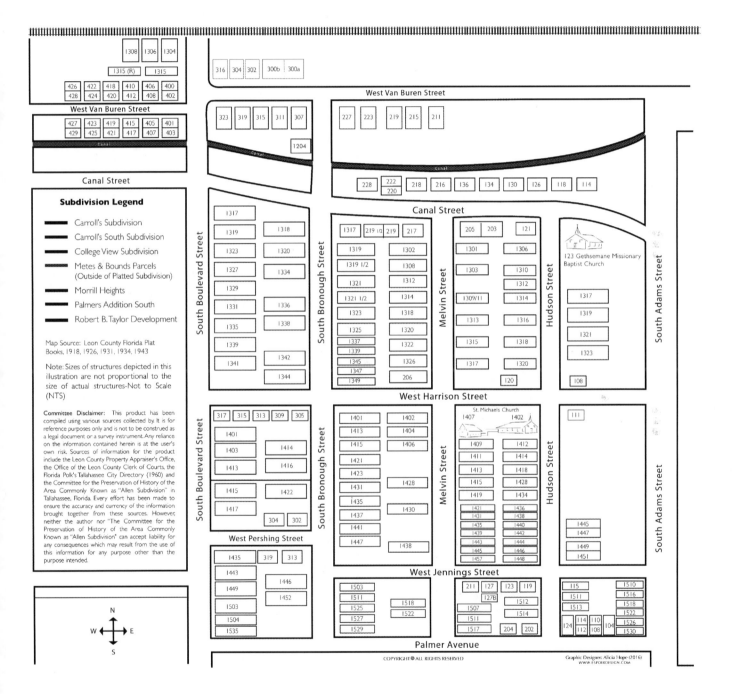

Map of Allen Subdivision by land developers, residences, family name, address, street block, home ownership and official subdivision. Image courtesy of Deloris Harpool

2

Homeowners by 1960

The Polk's directory lists ninety-two African Americans who had purchased their homes from earlier developers or owned their homes as of the 1960 directory publication date. The buyers collectively represented 45 percent of the 205 occupied dwellings in Allen at this time. Three fourths (75 percent) of the homes were purchased in the Carroll, Carroll South, and Morrill Heights Subdivisions from four Caucasian property owners, respectively: Fred Carroll Sr. and his wife, Clara; and J. T. Phillips and his wife, Elizabeth. The African American homeowners shown in the 1960 directory are listed below by the subdivision in which they bought their homes from the earlier developers. Some of them built their homes in these subdivisions.

Carroll Subdivision had twenty owners: Ary R. Brown; Gideon Clack; Phillip Young; William Lawrence; John Paramore; James Long; Stafford Evans; Leamus A. Henry; McKinley Wilson; Dora M. Jones; Alexander Henry; Willie R. Long; Eunice McCray; Ordray J. Washington; Melvin Beal; John Beal; Shelley Gavin; Martha B. Governor; Malissie F. Brazil; and Namon Mills Sr.

Morrill Heights Subdivision had twenty-two owners: Simon J. Young; Joseph Bines; Judge B. Kendrick; Johnny Brown; Hubert Brown; James Williams; Myrtle L. Ford; Willie Floyd; Moses G. Miles; John Steele; China B. Larkins; Arthur Holt; Nero Pender; L. Brooks; Luke Thompson;

Malicious L. Lincoln; Ora Young; A. Ralph Hoffman; Charles J. Stanley Jr.; Albert R. Crump; Parker Hollis; and Birdie L. Jones.

Carroll South Subdivision had seventeen owners: Dallas R. Madison; Rosetta S. Yopp; Walter F. Lamb; Willie S. Pittman Jr.; Eddie L. Smith; William Jefferson Sr.; Earl H. Boyd; Carrie T. Pittman; Corine Watts; Ada N. Harley; Ike Gilliam Jr.; Mary L. Hudnell; Willie C. Smith; Edna J. Anderson; Rosetta E. Edwards; Joseph Rosier; and Everett Flemming.

College View Subdivision had eighteen owners: Isaac Robinson; Phillip Dorsey; Bessie B. Ford; Georgia P. Long; Ernest Jones; Robert W. Matthews; Lula B. Young; Charles E. Weaver; Leroy F. Howard; Ollie R. Brown; Benjamin Long Jr.; Ezekiel Governor; Ethel C. Williams; Charles Young, Robert S. Sims Jr.; James E. Williams; Arthur L. Mobley; and Corine G. Smith.

Palmers Addition South Subdivision had twelve owners: Melvin R. Kyler; Ewing T. Brooks; Cecilia M. Mobley; Zeora R. Hercey; John R. E. Lee; George W. Conoly; Mathew H. Estaras; Allen P. Turner; Susie McLendon; Mary A. Larkins; Mamie E. Brazell; and Adolphus "A.D." Williams.

Taylor Development and Other Metes and Bounds Parcels (Not Platted as Subdivisions) had three owners: Roscoe D. Long; Jesse Ware; and Richard Ford.

Leon County Court records show that other residents had purchased homes in the Allen area prior to 1960, but their names were not listed in the 1960 Florida Polk's Tallahassee City Directory as were the homeowners listed above.

Life in The Community

It Takes a Village

Traditionally, Allen Subdivision has been characterized as a "good" or "strong" community. Although these descriptors may be debated by varying sources, the way that some experts describe a good or strong community incorporates characteristics of the Allen community.

One unknown author cites "shared emotional connection – shared history or experiences" and the "feeling of belonging" among measurable factors that yield a "sense of community."

Paul O'Neil states, "A good community is one where neighbors take pride in their living environment, respecting and supporting one another regardless of age, gender, race, or creed. He adds that a good community is "a cohesive, safe, confident, prosperous and happy place." Paula Bradshaw refers to a good community as "a happy place where children are collectively looked after and older people are valued." Vila Kilmurray emphasizes that a good community is one that "raises children together."

Mrs. Mary Harris, founder of Ma' Mary's Kitchen, holds great granddaughter, two months old S. Bronough Street resident, Debra Wanza. Courtesy of Debra Wanza Dabney

As penned by an unknown author of the April 25, 2017, Dunmore, Pennsylvania, news bulletin, "A strong community provides an environment of safety and security." From an economic perspective, this author suggests that strong communities "support … small businesses by shopping locally and choosing local venues over a chain." Kate Clifford expresses, "It's where people look out for and work with each other to make everyone's quality of life better."

All of the above characteristics can be attributed to the Allen community. The experience and value ascribed by its residents support the community's characterization as a wholesome place to live, raise children, and meet the needs of its residents. For over ninety years, long-term residents have expressed a deeply entrenched sense of caring, solidarity, loyalty, and pride in what for them became a large, extended family in Allen. Residents continue to describe Allen Subdivision as a "very close-knit community" and characterize their homeplace as "cohesive," "warm and loving," "caring," and "family-oriented."

Reverend and Mrs. Moses G. Miles share reading time with
daughter Andrea. Image courtesy of Florida Memory

Previous residents further described Allen as a community where "everybody knew everybody," "looked out for" and "took care of each other," and "got along." Some have described the area as a "nice and peaceful," "quiet" neighborhood, where there was no crime and, traditionally, people could leave their doors unlocked without any worries. They also have stated that Allen Subdivision was a place where "neighbors were like family" and where they "formed friendships for life." As in other African American communities, the residents in this geographic pocket of the city represented a range of occupations from lower-income domestic workers to higher paid chief university executives. Still, families bonded around common social challenges.

In spite of racial discrimination and a lack of the job and economic opportunities afforded their White counterparts, Allenites did not talk about or think about being sad or poor or being in poverty. They did not see themselves as indigent. For the most part, they were proud and happy souls, secure in their family, friends, neighborhood, church, social, and educational circles. Parents, elders, and mentors were hard-working people who carefully guided the thoughts of youth away from focusing on being poor. They provided a positive outlook with words like, "You got what it takes," "Just keep on trying," "Don't give up," "Work hard," "Don't let anybody turn you around," and "One day you're going to grow up to be somebody!"

Two words often expressed in most households were "make do." These words meant that people weren't to worry about what they didn't have but be grateful for and use what they did have. Elders also encouraged youth with statements like "Don't sit around pitying yourself," "Count your blessings," "Play the hand that was dealt you," and "Wherever there's a will, there's a way." No doubt, these lessons played a major part in Allen residents' being able to get their needs met legally and creatively, with dogged determination and with the expectation of a positive outcome.

The positive socialization of Allen residents and their children may be attributed to strong Christian teachings and beliefs. At early ages, children were taught to believe in and praise God and to recognize him as their creator, provider, and ruler of all human beings. They were taught to fear God and to adhere to the words of the Bible. Routinely they were advised that it was a sin to lie, to say bad words or to curse, especially on sacred church grounds.

Youth at Gethsemane Church were encouraged to accept Christ as their savior before age twelve. This process involved aspirants to sit on the 'mourner's bench' (front row pew) for one to two weeks. During this time, the candidates ceased normal social activities. They prayed day and night for God to forgive their sins. When led by the spirit, they were to leave the mourners bench, approach the church officials and acknowledge their acceptance of Christ as their savior. Church elders expected the candidates to shout out their joy in the church and in the neighborhood. Candidates were normally baptized at the Trueblood Swimming Pool or at a local lake. Not all youth kept their commitments after their conversion, but most as adults acknowledge having become more mature in their Christian walk and appreciating their earlier teachings.

For Sunday services, all church goers were to present themselves to God in their best – to dress up for the Lord. Easter was recognized as the day of Christ's resurrection and his atoning for the sins of the world. Youth and adults celebrated this sacred holiday each year. They proudly wore their new spring attire to Easter Sunday services.

Willie Washington, Lavern Washington, Melvin Beal, Nathaniel Grimsley and Christopher Adams pose in Easter Sunday Attire (Late 1970s). Image courtesy of Melvin Beal

Three generations pose in colorful Easter attire. From left to right: Mrs. Edna Anderson, grandmother "Big Mama;" Mrs. Leola Jefferson, mother; Nancy Jefferson, Leola's daughter; with Mrs. Dora Boyd, Edna's daughter, Leola's sister/Nancy's aunt. Image courtesy of Nancy Godette

Some of the Christian teachings were evident in practices reinforced throughout the day at home, school, and church. At school, before the beginning of classes, time was set aside for devotion to God and country. Via the school's intercom system, all classes participated in reciting the Pledge of Allegiance to the flag of the United States of America, a symbol of liberty and justice for all. The devotion sometimes included a prayer and a brief review of current events.

To "say grace" was required before meals at home and often at elementary school. The most commonly expressed grace for children was "God is great. God is good. And we thank him for our food. Amen." At night, before climbing into bed, children were taught to kneel at the bedside to pray. A commonly used prayer was "Now I lay me down to sleep. I pray the Lord my soul to keep. If I should die before I wake, I pray the Lord my soul to take. Amen."

The importance of family was engrained in the youth, beginning at an early age. They were expected to help around the house. When parents were at work or away from home, the older siblings took care of their younger sisters and brothers. This included helping to feed, bathe, dress, and groom the younger ones until they were able to carry out critical daily functions for themselves. The younger siblings were expected to do whatever they could to help. They understood and adhered to the authority given to the older siblings in charge.

In most homes, residents lived by the mantra that charity begins at home. As a part of the teachings in every household, all siblings were taught to love, share with, and when necessary, make sacrifices for one another. They were taught to not be stingy. They were expected to stick together, stand by one another, and be there for one another in good times and bad. The boys, in particular, were expected to protect their younger siblings, especially their sisters.

Allen boys were leery of guys who were not Allen Subdivision residents and who dated their sisters or other girls in the neighborhood. Willie D. Webster, initially considered an 'outsider' from the Tallahassee Springfield community, dated Mable Allison during their teen years. Says Mable, "What led to our 57 years of marriage was the way he treated and took care of me. We had a lot in common. My brothers and the Allen boys just got used to him." Willie says "It was just her person, and I just liked everything about her. Those guys didn't bother me. I saw a good woman and I went after her." Ultimately, the Allen boys accepted Willie as one of their own.

Youngsters were not to criticize one another or call anyone by a bad name. They were not to use curse words. They were not to hold grudges against one another. If one child offended another, at a minimum, he or she was to say, "I'm sorry" or "I beg your pardon."

The recipient was to forgive the offender, and the two were to make up with each other and move on as if the offense never happened.

Children were taught to respect their parents, teachers, and all elders of the community at all times. They were not allowed to talk back to or sass their parents, adult relatives, neighbors, or teachers or any persons of authority. Elders were to be addressed as "ma'am" or "sir." As a part of their spiritual development, Allen youth were taught and could readily recite the biblical verse, "Honor thy father and thy mother: that thy days may be long upon the land which the LORD thy God giveth thee" (Exodus 20:12 King James Version).

Neighbors willingly helped one another. They shared vegetables and fruits from their gardens and properties. They commonly fed their neighbors' children if they were visiting at mealtime. At times of illness or bereavement, residents prepared and delivered meals to their neighbors. They also shared items from their refrigerators and pantries. It was not uncommon or shameful for residents to send their children next door or across or down the street to borrow a cup of sugar, milk, flour, corn meal, eggs, or a stick of butter for their mothers to complete family meals or homemade desserts.

Parents, grandparents, and other elders in the neighborhood constantly reminded youngsters of how to treat and interact with others. One of their sage expressions, repeated throughout the neighborhood, was, "Do unto others as you would have them do unto you." They warned children with statements like, "Mind your manners" and "A hard head makes a soft back."

Regarding shaming others, bullying and participating in the spread of malicious rumors, they used multiple expressions geared toward appropriately interacting with others. To prepare for gossipers, they taught youth to be aware that "a dog that will bring a bone will carry a bone."

They also advised, "If you can't say anything good about someone, don't say anything at all." When children were unjustly provoked to the point of anger or pressed to respond angrily and quickly without thinking carefully, the elders advised, "Don't bite off your nose to spite your face," "Don't be so quick to speak," "Hold your tongue," "Hold your peace," "If you act the way they do, you are just as wrong as they are," or "Two wrongs don't make a right." If a friend reneged on a promise, the elders taught, "One monkey don't stop the show."

Children were expected to love and respect others and themselves. They were commonly taught to help others in need and to never look down their noses at anyone. They were encouraged to be humble and never think of themselves as better or higher than anyone else. Children were often reminded to begin or end requests for something from others with "please" and to begin with "May I." In addition, children were to express gratitude for gifts, favors, compliments, kind words, and other acts of kindness from others with the common expression, "Thank you!"

Business owners also played a key role in helping to rear children in the neighborhood. The Allen community was not absolutely flawless, and as in other neighborhoods, its children were occasionally naughty when they were out and about in the neighborhood. Based upon their observation of occasional mischief near their venues, business owners provided continuous oversight, guidance, and support for children. Like parents, these protectors warned, "At times, life will be hard" and "People will sometimes say bad things and tell lies about you." In cases of verbal abuse, all guardians taught youngsters thirteen empowering words: "Sticks and stones may break my bones, but words will never hurt me." Their words and expressions influenced attitudes of courage and strength in standing up to others and in dealing with life.

People who grew up, visited, or lived in Allen affirm that it was an admirable and safe place to live. In his assessment of life in the community, previous resident Napoleon Mills expressed, "We were protected. We lived a sheltered life. There were no bad people in our neighborhood, and there were no criminal incidents like you would frequently hear about in other sections of town." Mary Alice Allison Allen shared her impression: "Everyone was considered family. It was a nice neighborhood to live in. We knew all of our parents cared for and protected all of us."

Spare the Rod and Spoil the Child

Punishment for disrespecting elders or any misbehavior or disobedience took different forms. Parents sometimes used psychology to discourage bad behavior. For example, they might prohibit their children from watching television; having a favored dessert; playing with their toys; going out of the yard; leaving a designated room in the house; or attending movies, dances, or school activities. They might also give a kid more chores or withhold small change given on occasion for snacks and treats at the corner store. At times, particularly in public places, just a certain look from a parent or elder prompted immediate correction within the child.

The physical chastisement seemed more reminiscent for Allen informants. Parents and guardians spanked children with a firm hand to their backsides, thighs, or legs. At times, a disciplinarian used a belt or a switch to whip children. Where modern-day social scientists might consider whippings as child abuse, these guardians believed in the biblical message "Spare the rod and spoil the child." They were not concerned that the child or a neighbor might call the police. No parent bothered to report the other, as whipping children was viewed as tough love. It was commonly considered a necessary corrective measure to keep children out of future trouble and to keep them mindful of consequences of disobeying their parents, elders, or other authorities. Children were often ordered to 'go find a switch' – the very one that parents would use to whip the child. The residual pain, discomfort, or welts seemed very effective as lingering reminders.

Parents respected and supported one another in shaping the moral character of children in the neighborhood. They shared the same religious values and child-rearing practices. They allowed their neighbors, especially seniors, to discipline their children when needed. Most families knew the children who lived on all eleven cross streets in the neighborhood. Therefore, children could expect to be watched and disciplined on any street when their parents were not around.

Nellie Brown on Jennings Street and William Jefferson Sr. on South Bronough Street were parents who helped to keep their children, grandchildren, and others within their sight on the straight and narrow. They and other seniors might be seen spanking a child in the neighborhood without hesitation if the child misbehaved. These disciplinarians had no problem reporting to parents what they had heard and seen their children say or do and what they, themselves, had done to help keep the child in line.

Edna Anderson was one of the guardians of discipline who lived in the 1400 block of Melvin Street. She was known to be one whose eyes and ears would not miss a child's misdeeds. She was one of the elders in the community who knew everything that was going on with everybody. Youngsters were well aware of the importance of being on good behavior at all times around Mrs. Anderson, also known as "Big Mama." Moses Edwards shared, "I remember getting three whippings in one day. It was when I got spanked by two neighbors for misbehaving and another whipping from my mother when I got home."

Melissie Brazil, a designated mother of Gethsemane Church and babysitter for area children, was another stickler for good behavior among youth. From her porch and fenced yard at the corner of Harrison and Hudson Streets, she kept a watchful eye on all children passing by. With exacting power, she ended many potential squabbles and fights. She was often heard saying, "Don't y'all start no fightin' out there! Be good and go on home!" At the same time, her tough love was peppered with warm, nurturing affection for her "precious babies" in the neighborhood. Collectively, "Ms. Melissie," "Mr. Jefferson," "Ms. Nellie," "Ms. Anderson," parents, and other Village Builders were key in the development of good character among Allen youth.

Residents who held professional degrees or credentials also played important roles in shaping children's behavior and inspiring them to be successful in life. Guidance from these mentors included loving, nourishing, encouraging, and admonishing words. Mentoring was continuous because of the rapport that some residents who held professional positions established with their children's playmates or between teachers and their students living in the neighborhood.

Many of the neighborhood role models were prominent figures in their churches. Many were active in sororities, fraternities, non-Greek letter organizations, Masonic groups, social clubs, and other prestigious community service organizations. In some cases, merely the status, position, or employment status of professional neighbors influenced children to be on their best behavior in and outside the community. Parents welcomed and acted upon reports about their children's misbehavior from these caring neighbors. In fact, threatening statements like "I'm going to tell your mama" were words no Allen kid *ever* wanted to hear.

Individuals employed at Florida A&M University were among role models who, intentionally or unintentionally, helped to raise Allen's youth. These role models included, but were not limited to, Dr. John R. E. Lee, third President of FAMU; Reverend Moses G. Miles, a minister and FAMU dean of student affairs, who also posted bail for FAMU students arrested during the Civil Rights Movement; the Honorable Carrie Pittman Meek, FAMU college graduate and professor; Mathew H. Estaras, FAMU High School principal; Reginald Niles, athletics business manager; Alverta Morris, Librarian; Wilhelmina O'Rourke, FAMU High School English instructor, and her husband, FAMU Director of Food Services; and Dr. Eva C. Wanton, foreign language professor and, later, dean of FAMU undergraduate studies.

Additional FAMU employees who lived in the community and influenced good behavior and high aspirations among Allen youth included George W. Conoly, university administrator; Doris Mack, director of the FAMU Credit Union; Dr. Johnie Blake, FAMU professor of English; Doris Madison, home economics teacher at FAMU High School; John Steele, director of food services; Rebecca Steele, director of the FAMU choir; Ewing T. Brooks, farm manager in the Agriculture Department; Charles Weaver, university accountant; Dr. Charles Stanley Jr., FAMU education professor; Irma Kyler, FAMU High School business instructor; Willie Mae Miles, third-grade teacher at Lucy Moten Elementary School; Mable Sherman, high school music instructor; and John Boardley, professor of vocational technology, and his wife, kindergarten teacher in the FAMU N. B. Young Nursery School. Another mentor was Edward Debose, administrator in the FAMU Housing Department. Most of these college employees, along with the elementary, middle, and high school teachers, lived near the western periphery of the neighborhood on South Boulevard, West Pershing, South Bronough or near the southern end of the neighborhood nearest FAMU.

Other professionals who were not employed at FAMU also helped to steer youth along positive paths, either directly or vicariously. Georgia Long, well-known nurse and midwife, was among the noteworthy role models in Allen. Others included, but were not limited to, Nero Pender, widely known for his leadership roles in the Christian community, and his wife, teacher and Girl Scout leader at Bond Elementary School; Willie Ruth Brooks and Joseph Rosier, teachers at Pine Park Elementary School in Havana; Z. R. Hercey, teacher at the Original Lincoln High School (1865 – 1969); and Willie B. "Sweetpea" Estaras, teacher at the Original Lincoln High School and at Griffin Junior High School.

Other highly respected teachers in the neighborhood set positive examples for Allen youth and worked at other schools in the Tallahassee vicinity or in neighboring counties. They included, but were not limited to, Sarah Young, Pearl Crump, Estelle Pelham, Corine Allen, Gladys Herout, Lucinda Lawrence, Olivia Brown, Eugenia F. Brewington, Oma L. Homer, Blanche Gavin Holmes, and Joan Gavin Allen. These were teachers employed in Leon, Jefferson, Wakulla, or Gadsden County schools, collectively.

Parents at Work

Mondays through Fridays, most parents of the 2014 survey participants were at their low-wage, blue-collar jobs within walking distance of Allen. The Capital City Ice Plant on the corner of West Van Buren and Adams Streets hired some laborers from within the community. Arthur Mobley Sr. and Melvin Beal Sr. were long-term employees of the ice plant.

Melvin Beal, Sr., Mid-1940's employee of the Capital City Ice Company. Image courtesy of Melvin Beal

Historically, significant differences existed in the wages paid to Blacks compared to those paid to Whites. Even among educators in Florida, from 1890 to 1950, this pattern continued. Robert A. Margo reported that by 1950, "black teachers were paid less than equivalently qualified white teachers." He reported that the average annual salary of Black teachers in Florida was $2,643, 86% less than the average salary of $3,056 for public school White teachers.

Tacker reported that in 1965, among workers like cooks, maids and babysitters who provided domestic service in private households, "slightly more than half were Negroes." In this job category, the annual taxable wage average of all Florida workers was $770. In the US, it was $840 for Whites, which was 77% higher than the annual wage average of $770 for Blacks in Florida. In some cases, Allen parents held more than one job to make ends meet.

Many residents made the most of their skills and assets by operating businesses at home. Mattie Mobley operated a beauty shop in her Harrison Street home, and Ralph and Carrie Hoffman lived above their Ship Ahoy restaurant, where college students gathered for dancing and fast food on the floor below. Other women remained at home while running child-care, seamstress, laundering, or boarding-house services. For most community business owners, the workweek often extended to Saturdays, but their businesses generally were closed on Sundays.

In addition to some of the people listed as 2015 honorees on pages 48 through 55, some residents worked immediately outside the borders of the neighborhood. Some Allen residents were hired in bottling, packaging, and shipping operations at the Coca-Cola Bottling Company on South Monroe Street, on the east side of Adams Street between Oakland and West Harrison Streets. In higher-paying jobs outside of the northwest corner of Allen, men worked as station porters, baggage clerks, freight inspectors, or track-section maintenance crewmen for the Seaboard Railroad Coastline/CSX Company.

Within two miles of the neighborhood, residents found jobs in varying departments of the State of Florida, the City of Tallahassee, Leon County, Florida State University, the Capital City Country Club, the Duval Hotel, and the Florida Supreme Court. Some residents worked farther away from the Allen area in private homes as domestic workers, while a few worked at distant sites, including the Rose Printing Company in West Tallahassee and the Olin Gun Powder Company in Wakulla County.

Parents at Their Leisure

Up to the mid-1950s, the number of cars was limited. Families frequently walked to places they visited. Some residents rode the city bus, in taxi cabs or in cars with neighbors to places of interest. In their resting moments, parents often took advantage of the peace and solace offered at home or in the community. They regularly attended Sunday services and weekly Bible study.

To pass time, parents frequently sat on their front porches and talked with or visited their neighbors. Some parents played cards during their spare time. Men listened to boxing matches on the radio, especially those that featured the legendary Joe Louis. They also listened to baseball games broadcast on the radio, especially when Jackie Robinson played. He was a near-hometown favorite reared in Cairo, Georgia.

Most parents watched television when the one TV, with only one or two channels, in the home was available. The TV screen showed only black and white images. It was sometimes necessary to wrap the antenna ("rabbit ears") with foil to get a clearer picture and stronger TV reception. Along with listening to local news, adults found pleasure in watching gospel programs, evening TV comedy shows, and variety shows like *The Amos 'n' Andy Show, The Redd Foxx Show, The Flip Wilson Show, The Grand Ole Opry, The Lawrence Welk Show*, and *The Ed Sullivan Show*. Parents and their children also watched wholesome TV productions like *The Andy Griffith Show, The Roy Rogers Show, Gunsmoke*, and a small variety of other family-friendly shows. For parents and children, there was nothing more to watch on TV after 12:00 a.m., when the National Anthem was played and all programming ceased. The only thing viewers could see or hear was static, the broadcasting station's deliberate electrical interference, creating a fuzzy screen with a crackling sound.

Entertainment outside of the neighborhood for Allen adults included low-cost ways to relax while also putting food on the table. A few families owned cane poles, rods and reels, and crab baskets. Among their multiple ways to unwind, some residents drove approximately fifty minutes to the Gulf of Mexico to catch saltwater fish and blue crabs. They dropped their fishing lines and crab baskets from the Panacea Bridge. Favored freshwater fishing spots included Lake Munson, Lake Jackson, Lake Talquin, Natural Bridge, and the Ochlocknee River. When parents returned home, they sometimes shared the catch with family and friends during backyard fish fries and cookouts. On occasion, these events were held at Panacea Beach, popular for Fourth of July picnics and swimming. An added treat at cookouts was often homemade ice cream, hand-churned in a deep metal canister surrounded by rock salt to freeze the creamy, flavored liquid inside.

In the fall, parents took their children to the Leon County Fair to enjoy exhibits, carnival rides, shows, and sweet treats. Up to the late fifties, they also took their children to outdoor movies at the Capitol Drive-In Theater on South Monroe Street near the Leon County Fairground. According to Cinema Treasures, the Capital Drive-In opened in Tallahassee under the Talgar Theatres Company on July 15, 1949, with one screen and a four-hundred-car capacity.

Another popular spot that adults visited for affordable family entertainment was a drive-in theater north of Bragg Drive near the southern end of Pasco Street. At each theater, families watched movies on a supersized outdoor screen. The sound was transmitted through speakers that hung inside the driver's and front passenger's windows. Snacks were available at the central food pavilion on site.

Children at Work

The sale of pecans and soda (soft drink) bottles were common sources of income for Allen youth. Earl Washington gathered pecans at strategic spots as a way to ensure quick, seasonal earnings. He noted that the pecans at his secret spots became objects of near-territorial fights whenever someone else would come around and begin picking up the pecans he had shaken down. He explained, "I found secret pecan trees that I didn't tell anybody about. Every year, these trees were loaded! At these certain places, I could fill up a croaker sack of pecans all in one stop! That's where I got my money for the fair!"

Some youngsters raked yards, babysat, ran errands, or completed minor tasks for adults or businesses in the neighborhood. Lavern Washington fondly recalls sweeping floors and keeping things tidy in Charlie Davis's barbershop when he was a child. Washington reported learning valuable life lessons in the shop. As he explained, in addition to his cleaning duties, his role at the barbershop included "reading newspapers and discussing current events with customers, helping to settle contentious debates, and being the designated referee in intellectual aptitude challenges between barbershop customers."

On rainy days in the 1940s and early 1950s, as Dennis Jefferson recalls, he and other guys "made money pushing cars out of ditches" on the slippery hills in the community. During the 1960s, some of the boys worked as caddies at local golf courses. During the summers in the 1950s, boys and girls (mostly boys) worked on tobacco farms in Havana and Quincy, Florida. They were picked up on Adams Street by a large pick-up truck with a canvas that covered benches for employee seating in the bed of the truck. Some children rode under the benches, if additional help was needed. It has been reported that the adolescents earned about eighteen dollars per week, depending upon whether they picked tobacco leaves from stalks in the field, threaded them, or hung them in the owner's barn.

The young folks used their earnings for entry to the county fair, local dances and movies, sweet treats, toys, or bus fare. Their buying power was enhanced with green stamps issued with purchases at local grocery stores and redeemed at the South Monroe Street Green Stamp Store. While parents commonly traded their stamps for small appliances like irons, toasters, coffee pots, or kitchen utensils, the youth traded their stamps for items like transistor radios, roller skates, dolls, toy guns, or bicycles, depending upon the number of stamps collected and required.

Children at Play

Keith Miles celebrates his birthday at home with friends. Image courtesy of Florida Memory

At times, parents brought groups of their children's friends together for fun at their homes. Since space was limited in some homes, birthday parties and Labor Day and Fourth of July celebrations were commonly held in residents' yards. On special occasions, parents sponsored birthday parties or graduation or after-prom gatherings at the Jake Gaither Community Center or at the Dade Street Community Center. Some parents sponsored birthday parties at Gibbs Park on FAMU's campus.

Birthday party at home of Mr. and Mrs. Earl Boyd, 1441 S. Bronough Street. Image courtesy of Nancy Godette

For their day-to-day fun, children were not allowed to play inside the house and were required to be in the house before dark. They played on the front porch, in the yard, in the streets, in open lots, on the FAMU High School athletic field and playground, and at FAMU's Gibbs Park. At some point, inexpensive yo-yos and Bolo bats were found in every youngster's toy collection. Bid whist, tunk, and spades were the favored card games for teenagers or young adults. Old maid and go fish were popular for younger children.

Girls occupied themselves with dolls, playhouses, and line dances. "Here We Go Zudio" was a popular song accompanied by an early version of a line dance. Among other songs that kids sang were "Ole Mary Mack" and "The Clapping Song," as they faced each other making speedy, rhythmic claps against the hands of their partners. Teens practiced swing dancing with siblings, household mops, brooms, refrigerator handles and door knobs.

Many kids committed forbidden and dangerous acts for fun in the neighborhood, like running behind mosquito spray trucks. They often balanced on two large pipes extending across the canal on the north side of Canal Street (FAMU Way) at the intersection of South Bronough Street. Although prohibited by parents, this act was amusing for girls and boys. Those who walked or scooted themselves across the pipes, mastered the challenge without incident. The water trickling beneath the pipes was clear and shallow and it did not appear to pose a risk of drowning in this part of the canal. However, crossing the pipes did not always end well.

Cherry Lawrence recalled an unforgettable day in her youth when she encouraged a younger neighbor to walk across the luring pipes as a shortcut to a friend's house on Van Buren Street. She reported that the younger friend fell into the canal, got her clothes wet, and got sand in her hair. Lawrence added, "I was scared to death! I had to run water from the outside spigot at my house to get the sand out of my little friend's hair. Then, I had to sneak her into my house and dry her clothes in the oven to keep her mother and mine from finding out what I had done!"

Boys and girls played together in board, street, and yard games and sports. Among favorites cited by 2014 survey participants were kickball, dodgeball, jackstones, marbles, and Fiddle Stix. Both groups played hopscotch, checkers, dominoes, hide 'n' seek, and spin the bottle. They played handkerchief is walking, Simon says, one-two-three red light, four square, and three o' cat. In the 1950s and 1960s, teenagers delighted in listening and dancing to rock and roll and rhythm and blues sounds played on the radio by 'Cuz Kershaw.' Any teen who couldn't do the swing dance was "square."

Allen youth spent significant time playing gender-mixed games and competitive sports. Children of both genders played make-believe church, house, and school and raced down the paved hills of Allen on bicycles, roller skates, and skateboards. Both played softball, baseball, basketball, and jump rope. Particularly during their adolescent and teen years, the boys were more engaged in physical sports like football, basketball, and baseball. Sometimes, girls were allowed to play on the boys' selected neighborhood teams. Queen Bruton is one of the women from Allen who emerged as a star player on the FAMU varsity girl's high school basketball team.

Queen Bruton, third row - far left, poses with FAMU High girls basket ball team. Image courtesy of Queen Bruton

From Neighborhood Players to Distinguished Athletes

Allen Subdivision was known to have produced exceptional athletes. It is believed that the significant time spent playing competitive neighborhood sports is one of the factors that led to achievement in athletics for many Allen youth. Combined with their neighborhood activities, their individual gifts, talents, sportsmanship, and continuous family support, these youth were well-suited for athletic success. Excellent coaching at school also contributed to the preparation of Allen youth for high school and college athletic stardom.

Keith Miles is a former Allen resident who grew up in the upper 1500 block of South Bronough Street and who later became the director of communications at FAMU. By the mideighties, he was appointed as and became a highly venerated radio announcer for FAMU football games. This university leader expressed his recollection of friendly competitions in the midsixties and -seventies among the boys who lived at the top of the hill and the boys at the bottom of the hill in Allen. He stated,

> The boys at the bottom were really great athletes! They always won at whatever sport was in season, and we played them all! But the interaction between the two groups created lifelong connections, a special bond between us. To this day, we refer to each other as "another brother" or "sister" from "the Alley." No matter what fraternity or sorority we became members of or other organizations we joined, our connection to the Alley remained very strong.

Adolph Hicks grew up in the 1300 block of Melvin Street. He became a famed semi-pro women's basketball coach who also coached at four area schools. This noted athlete and sports leader shared,

> The guys in the neighborhood before me were my role models. They inspired me to be a strong competitor with good character. The young men from the Henry, Beal, Allen, Mills, Washington, Allison, Hinson and Madison families in Allen provided excellent leadership for me. What I learned early with them made me want to go beyond being a good athlete. It encouraged me to want to be a leader for other youth coming behind me.

At its June 9, 2007, neighborhood reunion, the Allen Subdivision family saluted individuals who achieved athletic excellence. In the 2007 reunion booklet, eighty individuals who lived in or grew up in Allen were cited as outstanding athletes. Neither the specific sports nor the years of highest achievement were indicated in the booklet for the individuals being celebrated. However, the collective accomplishments were reported by Allen residents as having been reached from as early as the midfifties to beyond the early eighties. The individuals cited in the booklet for athletic achievements included the following:

1. Alfred Allen
2. Keith Allen
3. Kenneth Allen
4. Toni Allen
5. Frank Allison
6. James "Chic" Allison
7. Larry B. Allison
8. Willie Allison
9. Mary Frison Avant
10. Allen Beal
11. Melvin Beal
12. Lawrence Beasley
13. Leroy Beasley
14. Barbara Bozeman
15. James Bozeman
16. Hubert Brown
17. Queen Hargrett Bruton
18. Kenny Burgess
19. John Chandler
20. Charles "Crickett" Clack
21. Harold "Papa" Clack

22 Buddy Colson
23 Nathaniel "Scaler" Colson
24 Willie "Sonny" Deas
25 Titus Deas
26 Phillip Dorsey
27 Georgette Ford
28 Patricia Ford
29 Tisa Ford
30 Willie "Grease" Governor
31 Ulysses "Big John" Harley
32 Raymond "Brother" Henry
33 Adolph Hicks
34 Alvin Hicks
35 Gerald Hinson
36 Terrence Hinson
37 Dennis "Denn" Jefferson
38 Donald Jefferson
39 Julius "Son" Jefferson
40 James "Bay-man" Jefferson
41 John "Dowee" Jefferson
42 Richard "Ricky" Jefferson
43 Thomas "Chuck" Jefferson
44 William "Boot" Jefferson
45 Samuel Jiles
46 Robert Kyler
47 Rowell Kyler
48 James "Cowboy" Lawrence
49 Robert "Bobby" Lee, Jr.
50 "Bay" Long
51 James "Buddy" Long, Jr.
52 James "Lum" Long, Sr.
53 Marcellus "Pete" Long
54 Roscoe Long
55 Samuel "Little Honey" Long
56 Ernest Madison
57 Carrie "Tot" Pittman Meeks
58 Bruce Mills
59 Napoleon Mills
60 Arthur Mobley
61 James Otis Mobley
62 Billy Morris
63 John Norwood
64 Elijah "Hook" Pittman

65 Samuel "Man" Pittman
66 Shawn Rivers
67 Edward Rodgers
68 Johnny "Bulldog" Rollins
69 Willie "Cheater" Rollins
70 Lorenzo "Teddy Bear" Russ
71 Robert "Rip" Russ
72 Moses "Shag" Simmons
73 Willie "Stacy-O" Simmons
74 Eddie Smith, Jr.
75 Edward "Smitty" Smith, Jr.
76 Evan Smith
77 Wendell Smith
78 Winifred "Dollarbill" Watts
79 Maud "Kuffie" Washington
80 Clyde "Zeke" Young

Makeshift Toys and Games

Like children in other neighborhoods, Allen youth collectively received Christmas gifts that commonly included dolls, dollhouses, bicycles, roller skates, toy cookware and dishes for girls. In addition to bicycles and roller skates, boys traditionally got basketballs and hoops, baseballs, bats, gloves, cowboy hats, cap guns, holsters, trains, toy soldiers, and BB guns. After Christmas, when parts of these items were either broken or lost, youngsters in Allen found creative ways to keep themselves entertained.

With great ingenuity, available natural resources, and discarded materials found in the neighborhood, Allen youth amused themselves at little to no cost. This was the case in the years reported as spanning from the 1930s through the early 1960s. Girls made paper dolls and doll clothing from newspaper, notebook paper, and pictures found in old magazines. Like the boys, girls made their own kites from sticks, old newspapers, and glue. Their handmade creations also included bottle dolls made from empty soda bottles, clothespins, and unraveled rope previously used to carry blocks of ice from the nearby ice house.

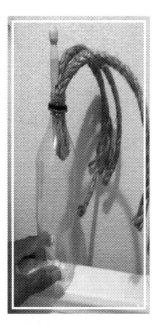

Bottle doll made from soft drink bottle, ice block rope and clothes pin. Image courtesy of Deloris Harpool

Girls used large cardboard appliance boxes to build their own sizable, crawl-in playhouses. The boxes were discarded from the Mays-Monroe Appliance Store after shipments of refrigerators, stoves, washers, and dryers to the South Adams Street distributor. The girls made mud pies and used leaves and grass for the imaginary food created in their playhouses. Betty Pittman reported, "We connected these big boxes to make fancy L- or T-shaped playhouses. We cut out windows and doors and made window curtains from fabric taken out of our homes."

Boys produced lightweight weapons for competitive games. Among their creations were pop guns made from the hollow bamboo reeds that grew abundantly in the community. With hand-trimmed bamboo sticks, the lads propelled chinaberries through the housing of the guns to deliver powerful blows to their opponents. Young men also crafted bows and arrows from arched sticks and sturdy string found around the house. They made slingshots from wide rubber bands and forked sticks gathered from trees and bushes in nearby yards and open fields.

For other inexpensive recreational devices, youth took advantage of broken toys and materials from home, fields, and area construction sites. With their crafty hands, they morphed wheels of broken roller skates into skateboards. With nails and with wire strings as steering gear, youthful engineers transformed two-by-four boards, old roller skate wheels, and bicycle seats into fancy go-carts, fit for speedy races down the hills of Allen.

The young innovators created low-cost springboards with concrete blocks centered beneath wooden planks that were ten inches wide, two inches thick, and twelve feet long. Dimensions of the springboards may have varied depending upon what the youngsters could find suitable for their needs. With one person balanced on each end of the board, the game started with each player using his or her feet and weight to cause the board to teeter. The object of this "thriller" game was for each player to use his or her weight to catapult his or her playmate as high into the air as possible, while the opposite player aimed to come down from the air on the board with equal or greater force. The board remained in motion as each player came down with increasing force on the board until one or both players no longer wanted to play or until a player lost his or her balance and fell off. Springboards were dangerous but simply exhilarating to Allen youth!

Jokes and Nicknames

Although the collective lifestyle of Allenites was not like that of affluent families, it certainly was characterized as one of much fun. Most Allen residents did not view themselves as being poor or downtrodden. Youngsters simply enjoyed life and one another with what they had. "Playing the dozens" or "signifying on one another" (making jokes about one another) was one of the ways residents brought merriment and laughter into their daily activities.

Jokes were not intended to be mean-spirited, harmful, or painful to others, nor were they received in a negative way. All involved knew that the jokes were simply intended to draw a good laugh. Statements in some jokes exchanged may have addressed life or cramped living quarters, like, "Your house is so small, I threw in a rock and *everybody* ran out with a hickey!" Another example is, "I stepped on a lit cigarette in your house and somebody screamed, 'Who put out the *lights*?'" with the variation, "… somebody screamed, 'Who put out the *heat*?'"

Other examples of witticism were related to residents' limited physical belongings. In this case, a joke may have included words like, "I saw somebody from your house kickin' a can down the street. I asked, 'What are you doing?' They said, 'Movin!'" Yet another went like this: "I looked down at your front doormat. It was so old, all it said was "Wel …?"

Nicknames were common in the community, as well. How some of the unofficial names came about was not determined in this review. Some were known to have been assigned based upon a physical characteristic, athletic ability, a humorous act, a personality trait, or affectionate utterances assigned to babies at birth. Others may have been derived from mispronounced, shortened, or altered forms of the recipients' official names. Most were simply pet names, reflecting endearing connection, community identity, and admiration for or comfort with the nicknamed person.

Residents of Allen responded positively to the alternative names assigned by their families and by the community. In some instances, nicknames were carried from childhood to adulthood. When called by the nicknames in a setting outside of Allen, adults would be amused and respond with enthusiasm. They would immediately recognize that the caller must be someone they had known for a long time in the past. The unique title would have been known only in their childhood or early days through the biological family, extended Allen family, or high school or college.

Listed below are some of the titles commonly known and accepted by recipients in Allen. It is acknowledged that some of the nicknames may be spelled incorrectly.

Al	Art	Babby Shack	Baby Doll	Baby Lu	Bamma
Bay	Bay Bay	Bay-man	Beesey	Big John	Billie
Bird Eye	Bobbie	Bobby	Bo Bo	Boot	Bruh
Brother	Buck	Bud Eye	Buddy	Bull Dog	Bunch
Cheater	Chic	Chicken Man	Chuck	Cimp	Cookie
Coota	Cowboy	Cricket	Dawh Wee	Denn	Dippy
Doll Baby	Dollar Bill	Duck	Dude	Ed	E. T.
Gin	Git	Grease	Honey	Hook	Jake
J. C.	Jeff	June Bug	Junior	Kebby	Kid
Kuffie	Leech	Lil Buddy	Lil Doll	Lil Mose	Little Honey
Lois	Loon	Luba	Lum	Ma Mary	Man
Mawh	M. G.	Mike	Mina	Minnah	Mitzi
Molly	Mr. Syp	M. T.	Mudeah	Nell	Nendi
Nick Nack	Nina	Nita	Noonie	Nouga	Pappa
Pat	Peanut	Pee Whiskey	Pet	Pete	Pippy
Pitt	Polly	R. C.	Rena	Ricky	Rip
Roll Hard	Roz	Sammy	Sang	Shag	Smitty
Snag	Snagalong	Sonny	Sonny Boy	Stacy-O	Striker
Sugar Bear	Suki-Nuki	Sustah	Sweet Pea	Teddy Bear	Tillie
Tina	Tot	Weed	Wild	Willie	Zeke

Mail-Order and Hand-Me-Down Clothes, Cardboard Soles, and Makeshift Closets

It is important to emphasize that life-styles and financial situations varied across the families in the neighborhood. Although most families experienced some of the same social challenges, financial difficulties and personal struggles did not manifest in the same way for all residents. In most Allen households, times were hard, dollars were few, and clothing was limited.

From the early 1900s through the 1960s, parents bought new clothing as needed in every season for their children. Although not the case for all households, children in many homes commonly received new outerwear three times a year: prior to the beginning of the school year, before Easter, and at Christmastime. For the latter, new, dressy apparel was needed for church. If the household income permitted, or if the mother was a seamstress or one who could make clothes from pattern books, the children received new or altered clothing more frequently. In other homes, some clothes were handed down from older siblings or neighbors. White employers commonly handed down their children's clothing for Allen Subdivision employees' children to wear. In addition, parents purchased mail-order clothes via Sears and Roebuck or Montgomery Ward catalogs. Traveling salesmen sold clothes in the neighborhood, as well.

Generally, there were three categories of clothing: Sunday clothes (the good clothes), school clothes, and everyday play clothes. Children were not allowed to play in their good clothes. After church or special events, they were instructed, "Get out of your church clothes and hang them up." In many homes, children owned two pairs of shoes: Sunday shoes and school shoes. A pair of sneakers might be available for gym classes and considered as everyday or school shoes. When the soles of their shoes began to allow direct exposure to the ground, some children inserted cardboard to cover the holes until their parents could buy new shoes.

Clothing closets were not available in every home, and space for clothing was limited. Fortunately, there was limited clothing to be stored per child and adult. For many residents, shoes were stored beneath the bed. In some homes, clothes were hung on the back of the door or high on an iron bar extended across one or two separate corners of the bedroom, depending upon the number of residents sharing and needing closet space in the room. In some homes, the makeshift closet was covered with a sheet to give the bedroom a neat appearance.

In other cases, the closet was a shallow space cut into or built off of the wall with an interior bar for hanging clothes. In such cases, clothing was concealed by curtains hung on a rod across the opening of the closet space. An armoire or chifforobe (pronounced "shifero" by early Allen residents) was sometimes available. Often used by parents, this free-standing cabinet had doors that enclosed shelves, drawers, and a space to hang clothes. A chest of drawers (pronounced "chestadraw" by some residents) stored underwear and sleepwear. A cedar chest or trunk in the room was used to store quilts, blankets, linens, or extra clothing.

Home Remedies

Residents could barely afford the services of family physicians when children or adults were injured or experienced minor ailments. From the early 1900s through the late 1960s, parents and grandparents addressed medical emergencies with practices passed down through the years. A blend of inexpensive compounds and elements found in or around the home were used for the medical quick fix. For example, the site of a bee sting was covered with wet chewing tobacco or snuff to draw out the venom. To stop bleeding, parents packed deep cuts and bruises with spider webs.

A foot punctured by a rusty nail was covered with fatback bacon and a penny. This combination was held in place by a tourniquet to extract potential infection. A sprained ankle was bandaged with a compound of red clay and vinegar. To treat the mumps, sardine oil or sardines were packed under and around the chin. This remedy was secured with a clean cloth covering the chin and tied at the top of the head. Colds and the flu were treated with a healthy dose of castor oil, cod liver oil or sometimes with a drop of juniper tar on a teaspoon of sugar.

When necessary, residents filled prescriptions and bought selected items from Baker's Pharmacy. Owned by pharmacist Wilmoth Baker and his wife, the South Adams Street establishment served Allen residents and residents of other Tallahassee communities from 1958 to 2003. Within a mile outside the southern border of Allen, the pharmacy supplied residents with items like prescriptions ordered by family physicians, bandages, gauze, rubbing alcohol, walking canes, and greeting cards. Petroleum jelly was available for medicinal reasons, and when hand lotion was not available, it was used as a lubricant to avoid dry, ashy skin. It was also used to treat chapped lips.

In addition to addressing the medical support needs of the community, Baker's Pharmacy was also a place for sweet treats. In one part of the establishment, the Bakers maintained a popular ice cream shop. Youth and adults frequented the north segment of the building for ice cream, milkshakes, fountain drinks, sundaes, and floats.

Superstitions and Myths

From the inception of the community, traditional beliefs and myths passed down through the years dictated how residents behaved in certain situations. Some Allen residents acknowledge that certain customs adopted during childhood have continued to drive their actions in the interest of avoiding bad luck or misfortune in adulthood. Some residents continued to believe into their adulthood that bad luck would befall them if they walked under a ladder, if a black cat crossed the street or path in front of them, if they swept the floor after dark, or if a woman sat her purse on the floor. Also, if two people approached a street pole together and one went around the pole to the right while the other went left ("splitting the pole"), both would have bad luck.

For good luck, a woman was to always carry black-eyed peas in her purse. For good or bad, if you dreamed about fish, someone you knew was or soon would be pregnant. If your left hand was itching, you were going to receive some money. Another myth was that a four-leaf clover would bring you good luck when found among grassy ground cover, which was rare. Some residents have reported spending long periods of time in childhood desperately searching for four-leaf clovers.

Certain myths related to an outlook of good luck if an individual followed certain traditions on New Year's Day. For example, if a person had money when the new year arrived, he or she would have money throughout the year. Similarly, if one ate collard, turnip, or mustard (dark) greens and black-eyed peas on New Year's Day, he or she would have good luck for the rest of the year. Also, if a male was the first person to cross the threshold into one's home on New Year's Day, he would bring good luck to the home.

Homegrown Foods

Allen residents relied heavily on fresh, homegrown foods. Few to no farm animals were in the neighborhood by the 1970s. However, from the early 1900s through the mid-1960s, many residents raised chickens, ducks, or quail for their daily supply of poultry and fresh eggs. These "yard birds" roamed freely in the neighborhood by day and found shelter in wire-mesh chicken coops by night. A few cows and goats grazed in grassy fenced or open yards and supplied fresh meat and milk. After 1935, residents bought feed and grains for their fowl and livestock at Gramling's Feed Store at 1010 Adams Street, next to the CSX railroad tracks.

Vegetable gardens, pecan trees, and a variety of fruit trees were scattered throughout the neighborhood. Colorful bounties from family gardens included collard, turnip, and mustard greens; cabbage; corn; sweet potatoes; squash; butter and green string beans; white-acre, purple, and black-eyed peas; okra; tomatoes; and cucumbers. For family treats, some residents were fortunate to have low-maintenance fig, plum, pear, pomegranate, date, or mulberry trees.

Residents picked free blackberries in nearby fields and in their yards. They also grew their own peanuts, watermelons, cantaloupes, pumpkins, and sugar cane and mutually shared their harvests.

Pecan trees held special value for residents. When thrashed during the fall, the nuts from the trees were an important source of income. Children and adults sold their pecans by the pound to the Hyman Myers Pecan Factory, located near the corner of Canal Street (FAMU Way) and Railroad Avenue (Wahnish Way). Especially during Thanksgiving and Christmas holidays, the nuts were used for homemade cakes, pies, cookies, candy, and healthy snacks.

"Yard Bird" on the Chopping Block

Within a stone's throw of the state capitol building, roosters in the neighborhood could be heard crowing each morning from the early 1900s through the early 1960s. Their companion hens were a special commodity for Allen households. Sometimes the female feathered animals would undergo a process that rendered them "dressed for the house." Whenever needed, residents would catch one of the yard birds, hold its neck tightly with a closed fist, and vigorously wring the fowl's neck until it broke. With great amusement, youngsters would laugh and mimic the "broke-neck chicken" as it flailed around on the ground, frantically flapping its wings until it became lifeless. Children watched as their parents held down the prey on a chopping block to cut off its neck with the sharp blade of the household axe.

The "yard kill" was then dipped in a pot of boiling water until its feathers were loosened and could be easily plucked from its skin. Once cleared of its feathers and internal organs, the fresh poultry was thoroughly washed, singed to clear all feather remnants, cut into sections, and washed again. Seasoned with salt and pepper, each poultry section was dipped in flour and deep fried in animal fat (lard) until it was golden brown.

Often served with collard, mustard, or turnip greens; green salad; cornbread; potato salad, mashed potatoes, or white rice with gravy from the pan drippings, this delicacy was commonly the center of the Sunday afternoon dinner table. In addition to a variety of cakes, the Sunday meal often included pound cake and apple, pear, or peach pie. Other common deserts included peach cobbler, blackberry pie, "blackberry doobie," bread pudding, or banana pudding.

At times, fried chicken parts were stewed in gravy, or the whole chicken was baked for variety. For even more variety, parts of the chicken were boiled with rice and other seasonings added to the pot. Although this savory dish may have been known to other communities and cities by a different title, to Allen residents it was called chicken purlow.

While chicken was served in different ways throughout the week, fried fish and grits were commonly served on Fridays. The most common dinner sides served throughout the week were white rice (normally served with gravy), leafy greens, and a variety of beans. Breakfast was served daily, including hot grits or oatmeal or cold cereal with milk; eggs; biscuits or toast; and bacon, ham, sausage, or salmon patties. Flapjacks, made only with flour and water, were pan fried until the edges were crisp and commonly served at breakfast with sugarcane syrup.

"Kool" Drinks, Meatless Sandwiches, and "Make-Do" Meals

Inexpensive drinks were readily available in every home, especially during the steaming-hot Florida summers. By the late 1950s, residents cooled their drinks with ice cubes from the refrigerator. Prior to this time, they used chips of ice from large blocks sold at the local ice house. At home, they created ice cubes by pouring water into small, ten-compartment plastic or metal trays and placing the trays in the freezer section of the refrigerator.

Getting frozen cubes out of an ice tray was often frustrating! The cubes seemed to stick like glue to the tray, even when room temperature water was poured over them to release them. Sometimes, the room temperature water would freeze instantly, causing the cubes to adhere all the more to the tray. Nothing was more maddening, especially when one was almost dying of thirst.

In addition to drinking a healthy glass of cool water, residents regularly consumed flavorful drinks at little expense. With a five-cent packet of Kool-Aid, a pitcher of water, and at least a half cup of sugar (probably more), residents could quench the thirst of the entire family. Poured in a glass filled with ice, this drink was quite refreshing and sufficient.

It is doubtful that Allen residents bothered to think about how blessed they were to have this popular "belly washer" available for just five cents per pack. According to Taylor Rock, this summertime cooler, named Kool-Ade prior to 1934, had been an American staple for nearly a century. Rock reports, "When the Great Depression began, the demand for Kool-Aid skyrocketed. It was a staple in practically every American home." Rock adds, "To help families in a time of extreme financial instability ...," the Perkins Company, Kool-Aid producer, "lowered the price from 10 cents a package to just five cents, and it stayed that way for years."

Certainly in Allen Subdivision for at least eighty years, Kool-Aid remained one of the cheapest and most commonly consumed drinks in the neighborhood. Offered in a rainbow of flavors like grape, strawberry, orange, raspberry, and lemon-lime, it was conveniently available at all of the neighborhood grocery stores. Whether residents knew this low-cost drink delivered a high punch of vitamin C is unknown. However, the tasty drink was often enhanced with other sources of vitamin C, such as fresh-squeezed lemon juice with lemon slices added for color. Sometimes residents preferred to drink plain lemonade. Whenever the budget permitted, they also used pineapple juice to enrich the flavor of their lemonade or Kool-Aid.

At times when neither Kool-Aid nor lemonade was available, desperation for a cold drink led to other creative solutions. At this point, some residents resorted to making and drinking a mixture called sweetenin' water. It was simply water infused with sugarcane syrup or sugar and served over ice. These thirst fixers were commonly consumed before ice tea became popular.

Lunch at home commonly included a drink and a sandwich. Sliced white bread with peanut butter and jelly (PB&J) or fried eggs was often plentiful, but lunch meat for sandwiches was not always there. In the absence of PB&J, chicken, tuna, ham, sliced turkey, hamburger, hot dogs, eggs, or baloney for lunch, residents satisfied their hunger in resourceful ways. They used white bread and any condiments or dairy products they could find in the refrigerator or pantry. Some reported having eaten mayonnaise, ketchup, mustard, butter, syrup, tomato, or cheese sandwiches. Some jokingly reported having eaten "air sandwiches," made with two slices of white bread and "nothing but air between."

While in college at FAMU, young adults from Allen could buy fast food for lunch, including burgers, fries, and a small variety of cold-cut and hot sandwiches at the Student Union. Occasionally, there were little to no funds available for lunch on campus. I recall,

> There were days when we just had to "make do." I remember many days when my friend, Freddie, and I would get hungry on campus, and we didn't have enough money to buy a sandwich. Refusing to walk home for lunch, with more afternoon classes scheduled, we sometimes combined our coins to buy one large order of French fries. We buried the fries with a mound of ketchup! That "mini" meal carried us through our afternoon classes and held us until we could get home to our moms' home-cooked meals.

Students from out of town shared some of the strategies they used to survive hunger. One (unnamed) FAMU graduate shared that she and two of her college friends lived together in a boarding house in Allen. She recalled one day when they were hungry and had little money to buy food. As she reported, "The three of us put our change together and bought a small pot pie at the Monroe Street Winn Dixie grocery store. We went back to our boarding house, cooked the small pot pie, and split it three ways."

According to another unnamed FAMU graduate, during the early to mid-1950s, FAMU served dormitory students early dinner on Sundays and gave them a choice of a baloney or cheese sandwich for a late-afternoon snack. As reported by this informant, since the cheese sandwiches were initially cold, the students heated the sandwiches in their dormitory rooms by pressing them with a steam iron. Still others have reported being lucky to have been invited to enjoy a full, hot, and hearty Sunday dinner with students who grew up in Tallahassee. Allen families were known to invite students into their homes for occasional meals, especially on Sundays.

Textured Hair, Burned Scalps, and Charred Upper Ears

Getting ready for special events marshaled feelings of great anticipation! Whether it was for church, an Easter program, a Christmas program, May Day, a school play or program, a date, or the prom, people got excited! They were going to be dressed up, mentally pumped up, and looking good! They would be dressed to kill or dressed to the nines. Their shoes would be shined and polished, their clothes would be fitted and pressed, and their hair would be freshly groomed. Once they looked in the mirror before stepping out the door, they saw people who were going to catch some eyes, draw attention, and get special compliments for how great they looked.

It was the hair that dampened spirits for some residents. For boys, grooming of the hair was not a big deal. Boys' sideburns, hair on the neck, or mustaches were either cut or edged and shaped by their dads, uncles, or brothers, or they did it all for themselves. At the neighborhood barbershops, for a small fee and (normally) entertaining wait time, boys and men could count on grooming with precision. Once they were old enough, the gents could shave their own facial hair with a razor blade or a straight edge. Of course, they might get an occasional jolt if they cut too deeply into the skin, but the pain of the tiny nick would soon fade away. The reward was worth it. Once the job was done, the face was smooth like a newborn!

For girls and women, hair was an issue! If they were not fortunate enough to be born with fine, wavy, or curly hair, the thought of getting their "hair done" was harrowing. Before hair perming chemicals were available and before trendy styles, wigs, and chic braids became popular, washing, detangling, combing, and straightening textured hair was no joke. Around the house, girls' moms, aunts, or older sisters did the honors. Or, once they were old enough, the girls groomed their own hair. For normal days, hair care required only deep combing, brushing, and occasional oiling and styling with braids or plaits, ponytails, or curls.

For special occasions, girls either received hair care at home or visited the beauty shop. At home, they often slumped over the bathroom or kitchen sink to get their hair washed and rinsed. It was dried under either a tabletop, dome-shaped electric dryer or a dryer with an expandable tube that blew hot air into a thick plastic cap that covered the hair. After their hair was dried, the girls often sat near the kitchen stove while their moms completed the final steps in this process. The mother would heat a straightening comb on a stove burner to get it hot enough to smooth every strand of her daughter's hair. In the same way, she would heat curling irons to a temperature that would create stiff curls that would hold for several days, aided by hair rollers. She would cut and curl a small portion of the hair for bangs over the forehead.

With specialized skills and equipment, the neighborhood beautician could do the same job faster, with greater precision, and with a more professional end result. But getting through the process under the hands of the beautician was not always a positive experience. I personally recall sitting under the unsteady hands of Ms. Williams, one of the neighborhood beauticians whose shop was on Harrison Street and who happened to be available when Ms. Mattie Mobley was not. Without drying my hair completely, she applied a hot comb to my wet hair, causing the hot water droplets to scorch my scalp. She often missed the edges of hair above my sideburns and charred my ears! In the middle of this traumatic experience, I told her, "Ms. Williams, I have to leave now. I'll be back. My mama told me to come home for lunch."

Obviously, having heard "Ouch!" so many times during my sitting, Ms. Williams knew I would not be back. She finished the job for which she had been paid. The price I paid was a stinging scalp; a few tears; and burned, crusted upper ears. After this experience, I told my mom, "I ain't *never* goin' back to Ms. Williams to get my hair done!" Although my hair looked great, the stress of it all nearly crushed my excitement about the upcoming Easter program at Gethsemane Church.

Early Bathing, Heating, Cooling, and Laundering

Until bathtubs and sinks were installed, residents took sitting baths in large aluminum tubs. They took sponge baths, using smaller face bowls or foot tubs made of tin. Kerosene lamps were used for lighting, and fireplaces were used for heating. In some homes, from the early 1900s to the early 1940s, free-standing wood-burning stoves were used for heating and cooking. Before families were able to buy fans for their homes, each dwelling was cooled by natural air flowing through exterior, latched, screened windows and doors.

Prior to the 1950s, before washing machines and dryers were affordable, residents cleaned their clothes by scrubbing them on wood-framed washboards with a corrugated scrubbing surface. After the scrubbing, they boiled the clothes in backyard wash pots. The clothes were rinsed in two large tin tubs and hung outside to dry on wire clotheslines extended across a portion of the backyard. Wooden clothespins kept the laundered items in place on the line.

One House, One Phone, One Party Line

The Southern Bell Telephone Company provided phone service and equipment to residents during the late fifties through the early sixties. Dial-up, desktop-styled telephones could be found in homes where they were affordable. With one phone per household, service was available via a shared party line assigned to multiple families within the same immediate geographical area.

The party line had multiple flaws. For one, it enabled residents to hear their neighbors' conversations. In addition, a user in one household was forced to wait until a neighbor had completed a call and cleared the line before initiating their own call. Residents often walked to area telephone booths to call a telephone operator for assistance in interrupting lengthy calls by their neighbors.

Early Transportation: We Walked a Lot!

Adams Street, Canal Street, West Van Buren Street, South Boulevard, and Palmer Avenue were the nearest city streets providing access into and out of the neighborhood. Getting out of the house and outside of the neighborhood for fun and other needs was sometimes a necessity. Fortunately, the location of Allen afforded its residents immediate access to downtown shopping, to area commercial and business districts, and to other places of interest. As provided in oral testimony, most residents walked to varying sites from the early 1900s up to at least the 1960s.

Although it was common for some families to own at least one vehicle, other residents rode the city bus, rode with others who owned vehicles, or walked to the downtown shopping district, the Leon County Health Clinic on East Gaines Street, grocery stores outside of Allen when necessary, or other venues. Parents often walked to work at places near Allen. On occasion, adults utilized the Quick Service Taxi business operated from the Macomb Street office of owner Charlie Hudley. Melvin Beal Sr., resident of 1312 Melvin Street; James Williams, of 211 West Jennings Street; and Arthur Givens, of 1313 Melvin Street, were three of the taxi subcontractors stationed and available from their homes in Allen.

College students walked from Allen boarding houses and apartments to FAMU. Elementary and high school students walked to school if they were enrolled at Lucy Moten, FAMU High, or the St. John's School in Smokey Hollow. County school buses were available to carry students to schools outside of Allen, particularly before full integration of Leon County schools.

Prior to the passage of the Civil Rights Act of 1964, Blacks and Whites used separate public facilities. Blacks in Tallahassee could only attend movies, swimming, and other recreational or leisure activities designated for Blacks only. If no ride was available, Allen youth and teenagers frequently walked one mile north from Allen's northwest edge to the Leon Theater near the corner of West Tennessee Street and Wahnish Way (the former Railroad Avenue).

Another two miles farther, they walked to the all-Black Dade Street Community Center. There, they took advantage of roller skating, weekend dances and parties, card games, pool, basketball, and other indoor games. Directly next door to the Dade Street center, near Alabama Street, was the Robinson Trueblood Swimming Pool for summer recreation and swimming lessons. When rides were available, teens also visited the Jake Gaither Park Community Center on Stafford Drive for fun and recreation on the south side of town.

Teens also walked to attend basketball games, dances, and other activities at FAMU High and at the Original Lincoln High School within a mile north of the Leon Theater. Young adults and college students often walked to the Blacks-only American Legion Home, a popular dance spot on Brevard Street. Allen teens and their parents walked to the city's Centennial Field for baseball games and annual rivalry football games between FAMU High School and the Original Lincoln High School. The ball fields were replaced by a segment of the current Cascade Park at the corner of Monroe and Bloxham Streets. Prior to the South Monroe Street location of the county fair, parents and their children walked to the fair when it was held in the Allen vicinity, near the corner of Railroad Avenue (Wahnish Way) and Canal Street (FAMU Way).

Bustling Black-Owned Business Community

By the time that Allen Subdivision was fully developed, its robust body of African American–owned businesses had become the crown jewel of the neighborhood. Until the mid-1960s, segregation was the order of the day, and Blacks had limited choices of venues where they could shop or seek services. Between the 1940s and the mid-1980s, as residents of the community launched businesses to meet the needs of others in the area, Allen emerged as a functional and vibrant economic center for its residents. It became a thriving, significantly self-contained community. It featured a wide range of products and services available in buildings and private homes within a mile's radius of the geographic center of the neighborhood.

By 1980, more than ninety African American–owned businesses were flourishing along West Van Buren, Canal (FAMU Way), West Harrison, West Pershing, South Adams, Melvin, South Bronough, and South Boulevard Streets. A sizable portion of the businesses were owned and operated by individuals without licensure or certification. Very few were publicly listed. The owners utilized their skills, trades, and wit to supplement their family incomes while providing affordable, robust products and services for area residents. They used their personal equipment, vehicles, vacant rooms, or extra space in their homes as necessary resources.

The need for interdependence between the business sector and the residents of the community was understood. Sticking together and supporting one another was a way of life. Businesses depended upon word-of-mouth communication by loyal neighbors, students, and patrons from outside of the neighborhood for ongoing promotion and survival. The convenient location and visible presence of the businesses near a university also contributed to ongoing advertisement of the products, goods, and services offered.

Love, caring, respect, and protection abided between business owners and residents in the community. Many business owners lowered costs, allowed credit accounts, and gave freely to Allen residents in need. Vendors helped to guard one another's property, although break-ins and vandalism, if any, very rarely occurred. Customers from outside of Allen were also important to the sustainability of Allen venues. As residents and others patronized the businesses with unwavering loyalty and the businesses supported one another, the venues grew and became more sustainable. Collectively, these partners became a formidable economic engine.

The source of the businesses' funding to launch their operations was not determined. No African American banks or lenders were in the Allen community or in Tallahassee to the knowledge of the author or other informants queried as of 2015. Residents of the community speculate that funding may have come from multiple and varied sources: some owners' personal savings, extra employment, loans under the G. I. Bill, family inheritance, heir property sales or collateral, and the rental of rooms in the business owners' personal homes.

Based upon speculation from other residents, start-up, maintenance, and continuation funding for Allen entrepreneurs may have come through loans from local White-owned banks. As reported by other informants, other possibilities included gifts or loans from Caucasian employers or friends and funds secured with Caucasian sponsors or cosigners. One resident stated that his father launched his construction business with extra funds from raising and selling hogs. Another idea posited included possible funding from activities like the sale of moonshine or alcohol.

In addition to the influence of eminent domain in the 1980s, residents of Allen reported that their parents or relatives closed their businesses for varying reasons. Some residents said their parents were forced to end their businesses due to declining health. One resident reported that her father closed his business because holding a full-time job while managing a small business became too much for him to handle. The wife of another business owner reported that, when she graduated from college, she and her husband secured higher-paying jobs with fringe benefits that far outweighed the minimal profits from her husband's small business. Yet another owner reported that the cost of general liability and workman's compensation insurance made it impossible to stay in business and maintain reasonable profits.

The venues owned by African Americans in Allen included, but were not limited to, grocery stores; fish, seafood, and meat markets; beauty and barber shops; cafés and dinettes; and bars, clubs, and lounges. The burgeoning district also included child-care centers; tailoring, seamstress, and alterations sites; upholstery, jewelry, shoe, and electronics repair shops; a dry cleaners venue; a florist; taxi services; and a service station and auto repair shop. Women managed over 50 percent of the businesses, including boarding houses, restaurants, beauty shops, and child-care centers. Boarding houses operated in homes throughout the neighborhood and made up the greater share of businesses in the area.

Campus Cleaners, owned by Otis and Sybil Mobley. Image courtesy of son, James O. Mobley

The list below provides brief descriptions of some of the African American–owned enterprises that existed in Allen during its most vibrant years, between the 1940s and the mid-1980s.

AD's Café and Motel, located at the corner of Boulevard and Van Buren Streets, offered limited prepared food and snacks. More significantly, the two-story facility offered short-term lodging for African American travelers.

AD's Grocery Store, at 316 West Van Buren Street, provided a variety of staples and snacks in the northwest section of the neighborhood. The owners of the small store,

Adolphus Williams and his wife, were entrepreneurs who also owned AD's Café and Motel and the Savoy Club, located on West Van Buren Street.

Anderson's Childcare provided babysitting and child-care services for area Tallahassee residents, including FAMU faculty, students, and administrators. Edna Anderson, owner, operated this business in her home at 1438 Melvin Street.

Ben's Grocery Store, in the 1300 block of Melvin Street, offered a small variety of staples and sweet treats. It was also popular for the sale of beer, wine, cigars, cigarettes and wood.

Bill's Seafood, located at 136 Canal Street, was also called Mr. Sip's store and attracted customers living in and outside of Allen. It provided a variety of fishes, including but not limited to bream, mullet, catfish, trout, shrimp, and wild game.

Charlie Davis Barber Shop and **Hillside Barber Shop** were operated on Canal and Pershing Streets, respectively. Their respective owners, Charlie Davis and Eddie Barrington, groomed boys and men with haircuts and clean shaves. Each site was a popular gathering place where men discussed sports and athletics, exchanged ideas, held informal debates, and shared updates about people, current events, and politics.

Crump's Store was conveniently located in the heart of Allen at the corner of Melvin and West Harrison Streets. The owners, Albert and Pearl Crump, sold a wide variety of products and goods. They offered popular staples, including milk, eggs, cheese, bread, butter, sugar, rice, grits, flour, corn meal, canned goods, and cold cuts. Among other items, cigarettes, cigars, chewing tobacco, and snuff also were available. Kerosene and matches were available for heating and cooking needs in neighborhood homes. Children frequently visited Crump's, Henry's, and A. D.'s stores for tasty treats like ice cream, popsicles, dreamsicles, fudgesicles, cookies, cakes, pastries, candy, bubble gum, potato chips, pork rinds ("skins"), and soft drinks ("soda water"). Popular candies included Baby Ruths, Snickers, Hershey bars, Butterfingers, Zeros, Almond Joys, Paydays, Sugar Babies, Sugar Daddies, BB Bats, M&Ms, Mary Janes, and peanut butter cups.

Dupont's Meat Market, located at the intersection of West Van Buren and South Adams Streets, supplied meats, including poultry and fresh, cut-to-order beef and pork.

Fountainette, an after-school and -event gathering spot, was located at the corner of West Pershing and South Boulevard Streets. With a jukebox and a dance floor, this lounge offered high school and college student entertainment. Foods included hot meals, snacks, and soft drinks for youth. After changing management and clientele, the lounge offered beer and wine for adults.

When the Fountainette closed, Weser Khufu took ownership of its building to offer a full complement of construction services through his **Pyramid Construction Company**.

Site of the Fountainette building under renovation by the new business occupant, Weser Khufu, owner of Pyramid Construction Company. Image courtesy of Weser Khufu.

Henry's Grocery Store was popular for the sale of items similar to those sold at Crump's Store. Raymond B. Henry and his wife Leamus operated their store at the corner of South Bronough and Canal Streets. Children flocked to their store for snow cones topped with crushed pineapples and sweet cream, a unique commodity and a huge summertime hit!

Peppermint Patio was a prominent nightclub on Canal Street that flourished from the late 1950s to the early 1960s. It was similar in its offerings but different in physical structure from the Savoy Club. Owned by Leroy and Sophia Ash, this establishment brought to the Black community the concept of a club without a roof. The patio was built with a six- to eight-foot-tall wooden-plank fence that enclosed a band stage and a spacious concrete floor for dancing. The only covered segments of the club were the restrooms, a bar where alcoholic beverages were served, and a kitchen where meals were prepared. Tables and chairs were placed around the uncovered open floor to accommodate seating for club guests. Entertainment was provided during the spring and summer months by varying performance groups.

Pittman's Boarding House offered room and board for scores of college girls seeking off-campus housing through many years. The two-story, thirteen-room, wood-frame house was owned by Willie and Carrie T. Pittman, parents of the late honorable congresswoman Carrie Pittman Meek, the youngest of the Pittmans' twelve children. Located at 1447 South Bronough Street, one block away from the FAMU campus, the boarding house was a symbol of ingenuity, pride, creative economics, and prosperity to area neighbors. It was one of over ten rooming houses operated by Allen residents. A commemorative marker erected in 2020 at the corner of Jakes and Patterson (previously, Jennings) Street and South Bronough Street denotes the site where the demolished home once stood. Due to previous COVID-19 concerns, the unveiling of the marker was postponed until 2022. **See two-story home in background of image on page 33.**

Roberta's Florist offered flowers, floral arrangements, and ornamental plants. Operated by Roberta Barrington, this establishment was popular for arrangements of bouquets and corsages required for weddings, cotillions, school productions, and other special events. It also was a Tallahassee go-to spot where patrons ordered fresh flowers for bereaved families and funerals.

Savoy Club was a popular nightclub on West Van Buren Street owned by Aldophus Williams and his wife. In the 1960s and 1970s, the Savoy was a flourishing venue, featuring live entertainment, a jukebox, dancing, hot meals, and alcohol for customers ranging from college students and young adults to more seasoned club goers. Local clientele and traveling club goers filled the Savoy wall to wall every weekend.

Ship Ahoy, owned by Alphonso Ralph Hoffman Sr. and Carrie Hoffman, was a popular restaurant and lounge at 1540 South Adams Street that the Hoffmans started in 1952. Their venue stood on the corner of Adams and Palmer Streets, directly across the street from FAMU. This venue offered lounging, meals, alcoholic beverages, and dancing. Its clientele included college students, young and more mature adults, and local and traveling customers. In its early stages of operation, the restaurant served meals in its first-floor main dining room; in its Blue Room; and, for special occasions, on its roof. Attached to the Blue Room was a stairway that led guests to the rooftop, where they lounged and received meals delivered from the kitchen via a dumbwaiter.

Ernest and Carrie Hoffman, front left and center, relax with Colonel Willie and Mrs. Thelma Jenkins (rear center) and other friends on the Ship Ahoy rooftop. Image courtesy of son, Dr. Ernest Hoffman, Jr.

The Hoffmans housed their family in a segment of the second floor of their building and students in another section on the second floor. In the same two-story building, these entrepreneurs created a multiplex that, over time, became a site for other Black-owned businesses, including radio repair, pizza and barber shops, and other Black business occupants. Although the building was destroyed by fire in 1991, it was up and running again by December of 1994.

Ernest Hoffman, owner, at the Ship Ahoy Restaurant. Image courtesy of son, Dr. Ernest Hoffman, Jr.

Tucker's Service Station operated at the corner of Adams and West Harrison Streets. Known by area residents as the neighborhood service station, this business provided fuel, maintenance and repair for motor vehicles, as well as kerosene for home heating.

Presented in the table below is a detailed listing of over ninety African American–owned businesses known to have existed in Allen Subdivision from the mid-1940s to the mid-1980s. Some of the businesses occupied the same physical space as others but within different time frames. The venues are listed below by name, owner(s), street address, and type of operation.

TABLE 1. African American–owned businesses in Allen Subdivision, 1946–1980

#	Name of Business	Owner(s)	Street Address	Type of Business
1	AD's Café and Motel	Adolphus D. Williams	311 W. Van Buren Street	Restaurant/motel
2	AD's Grocery Store	Adolphus D. Williams	316 W. Van Buren Street	Grocery store
3	Allison's Grocery Store	Henry Allison	136 Canal Street	Grocery store
4	Anderson's Childcare	Edna Anderson	1438 Melvin Street	Babysitting
5	Artistic Barber Shop	Harold Clack	121 Canal Street	Barber shop
6	Artizan Beauty Parlor	Everett and Naomi Fleming	111 W. Harrison Street	Beauty shop
7	Askew's Beauty Parlor	May F. Askew	313R W. Harrison Street	Beauty shop
8	Askew's Dinette	Willie C. Askew	205 Canal Street	Dinette
9	Beal's Taxi Service	Melvin Beal Sr., subcontractor, #13, Quick Service Cabs	1312 Melvin Street	Taxi service
10	Ben Washington's Grocery Store	Benjamin and Audrey Washington	909 Melvin Street	Grocery store and wood sales
11	Bill's Fish Market	William "Sip" Long	205 Canal Street	Seafood market
12	Blue Ribbon Café	Cora Moore	203 Melvin Street	Restaurant
13	Blue Ribbon Café	Margaret Hodges	203 Melvin Street	Restaurant
14	Bob's Barbershop	Robert Moore	1532 S. Adams Street	Barbershop
15	Brooks' Newspaper Distribution and Collections	Ewing T. and Henry Marcellus Brooks, Subcontractors, John Davis and *Tallahassee Democrat* Newspaper	1443 S. Boulevard Street	Newspaper distribution and collections
16	Brooks' Room Rentals	Ewing T. Brooks	1443 S. Boulevard Street	Room rentals
17	Brown's Boarding House	Nellie Brown (Hubert Brown, son)	127 W. Jennings Street	Boarding house
18	Brown's Alterations	Susie Brown (Hubert Brown Sr., husband)	127 1/2 W. Jennings Street	Alterations
19	Campus Cleaners	James and Sybil Mobley	312 W. Pershing Street	Cleaners/clothier
20	CE's Beauty Shop	Clara Allen & Willie Allen	401 W. Van Buren Street	Beauty shop
21	Chick's Fruit Stand	James H. Allison	1413 Melvin Street	Fruit market
22	Clack's Laundering and Baby Sitting	Alice Clack	121 Canal Street	Babysitting and laundering

23	Crump's Grocery Store	Albert and Pearl Crump	1402 Melvin Street	Grocery store
24	Colson's Beauty Shop	Jeanette/Walter Colson	319 W. Van Buren Street	Beauty shop
25	Davis Barber Shop	Charles Davis	136 Canal Street	Barbershop
26	Dora's Ceramics	Dora Boyd (Earl Boyd, husband)	1441 S. Bronough Street	Ceramics sales
27	Dorsey's Alterations	Fleta Dorsey (Freddie Dorsey, husband)	1418 W. Van Buren Street	Alterations and seamstress
28	Dupont's Meat Market	George D. Dupont	1100 S. Adams Street	Meat market
29	Econo Wash Laundromat	Dallas S. Winchester	316 W. Pershing Street	Laundromat
30	Edwards' Room Rentals	Rosetta Edwards	1439 Melvin Street	Rooming house
31	Ford's Rooming House	Lula Ford	1503 S. Bronough Street	Boarding house
32	Givens Taxi Service	Arthur Givens, subcontractor, Quick Service Cabs	1313 Melvin Street	Taxi service
33	Greene's Insurance Agency	Arnett Greene	1530 S. Adams Street	Insurance agency
34	Hawaiian Grille	Isabelle Robinson	203 Canal Street	Lounge
35	Hawaiian Grille	Benjamin Washington	203 Canal Street	Lounge
36	Hawaiian Grille	Cora Moore	203 Canal Street	Lounge
37	Hawaiian Grille	Margaret Hodges	203 Canal Street	Lounge
38	Henry's Grocery Store	Raymond B. and Leamus Henry	147 Canal Street	Grocery store
39	Henry's Boarding House	Raymond B. and Leamus Henry	1317 S. Bronough Street	Boarding house
40	Hercey's Plumbing	Zeora Hercey	1503 S. Boulevard Street	Plumbing
41	Hillside Barber Shop	Edward Barrington	321 W. Pershing Street	Barbershop
42	Hillside Beauty Shoppe	Eddie Barrington	311 W. Pershing Street	Beauty shop
43	Hillside Fountainette	Leonard D. Foote	320 W. Pershing Street.	Lounge
44	Hinson's Grocery Store	Prince Hinson Jr.	1402 Melvin Street	Grocery store
45	Hoffman Apartments	Alphonso R. and Carrie Hoffman	1540 S. Adams Street	Apartment rentals
46	Hoffman's Nursery	Alphonso R. and Carrie Hoffman	104 W. Palmer Avenue	Child care
47	Holjack's Barber Shop	Parker Hollis and Bosie Jackson	1532 S. Adams Street	Barbershop
48	Homer's Laundering and Babysitting	Mary Homer	1317 Hudson Street	Laundering and babysitting
49	House of Moses	Moses McCray	320 W. Pershing Street	Lounge
50	Jefferson's Room Rentals	Leola and William Jefferson	1437 S. Bronough Street	Rooming house
51	Jet Radio TV and Sound Shop	Ethel H. Taylor	1534 S. Adams Street	Radio/TV repair
52	Johnson's Peanuts	Daniel Johnson	1320 Melvin Street	Peanut sales

53	Johnson's Shoe Repair	Walter and Ora Johnson	1536 S. Adams Street	Shoe repair
54	Kendrick's Rentals	Judge B. Kendrick	123 Jennings Street	Rooming house
55	Lamb's Boarding House	Evelyn Lamb (Walter Lamb, husband)	1421 S. Bronough Street	Rooming house
56	Lamb's Day Care	Evelyn Lamb	1421 S. Bronough Street	Rooming house
57	Lou's Cafe	Lucinda Williams	218 Canal Street	Restaurant
58	Malissie's Childcare	Malissie F. Brazil	120 W. Harrison Street	Babysitting
59	McClendon's Property and Room Rental	Susie McClendon	302 W. Pershing Street	Property and room rental
60	McClendon's Western Union Services	Susie McClendon, subcontractor, Western Union	302 W. Pershing Street	Money transfer
61	Mills Hauling	Namon Mills Sr.	1310 Hudson Street	Pick up/delivery
62	Mobley's Beauty Shop	Mattie Mobley	309 W. Harrison Street	Beauty shop
63	Mobley's Boarding House	Arthur and Mattie Mobley	309 W. Harrison Street	Room rentals
64	Mobley's Rentals	James and Sybil Mobley	312 W. Pershing Street	Room rentals
65	Moses's Pizza Fountainette	Moses McCray	320 W. Pershing Street	Restaurant
66	Paramore's Rentals	John Paramore	136 Canal Street	Rental property
67	Pearlie's Rooming House	Pearlie Stretching Lyons	1413 S. Bronough Street	Rooming house
68	Peppermint Patio	Sophia Ash	138 Canal Street	Bar and lounge
69	Pender's Boarding House	Nero Pender	1518 Melvin Street	Rooming house
70	Pittman's Boarding House	Carrie T. Pittman	1447 S. Bronough Street	Boarding house
71	Pyramid Construction	Weser Khufu	320 W. Pershing Street	Construction/masonry
72	Quality Upholstery	Robert L. Roulhac	1536 S. Adams Street	Furniture upholstery
73	Rosetta's Sewing and Alterations	Rosetta Edwards	1439 Melvin Street	Seamstress and alterations
74	Roberta's Florist	Roberta Barrington	324 W. Pershing Street	Florist
75	Sam's Restaurant	Virginia Long Abner	203 Canal Street	Restaurant
76	Savoy Club	A. D. Williams	311 Van Buren Street	Nightclub
77	Scott's Fish Market	David Moore (Mgr.)	205 Canal Street	Fish market
78	Ship Ahoy	A. Ralph and Carrie Hoffman	1540 S. Adams Street	Restaurant/lounge
79	Smith's Jewelry Shop	Eddie L. Smith	1431 S. Bronough Street	Watch/jewelry repair and sales
80	Smith's Newspaper Distribution and Sales	Eddie L. Smith, subcontractor, Pittsburg Courier	1431 S. Bronough Street	Newspaper distribution/sales
81	Square Deal Construction	Raymond Bellamy and Marian Watson	1530 S. Adams Street	Construction

82	Tucker's Standard Oil Station	Fred Tucker	1404 S. Adams Street	Service station
83	Washington's Construction	Abraham Washington	1337 S. Bronough Street	Brick masonry and plumbing
84	Washington's Rooming House	Estelle Washington	216 Canal Street	Boarding house
85	William's Boarding House	Olivia Williams	211 W. Jennings Street	Boarding house
86	William's Beauty Parlor	Olivia Williams (James Williams, husband)	211 W. Jennings Street	Beauty shop
87	William's Curly Way Beauty Shop	Madeline Williams	305 W. Harrison Street	Beauty shop
88	Williams' Taxi Service	James Williams, subcontractor, Cab #47, Quick Service Cabs	211 W. Jennings Street	Taxi service
89	Yopp's Boarding House	Rosetta Yopp	1415 S. Bronough Street	Boarding house
90	Young's Property Rentals	Phillip Young	126 Canal Street	Property rental
91	Young's Rooming House	Mamie Young	115 W. Jennings Street	Property rental

Note: This table includes the African American-owned businesses brought to the attention of the author as having existed between 1946 and 1980 within the boundaries of the community known by its residents as Allen Subdivision. *Sources:* Polk's Tallahassee City Directory, Polk's Directory of Householders, Occupants of Office Buildings and Other Business Places, Including a Complete Street and Avenue Guide, R. L. Polk & Co., Publishers, 1946–1980, and Allen Subdivision residents, business owners, relatives and/or customers of business owners, 1946–1980. Research by Deloris Mills Massey Harpool and Cherry D. Lawrence.

For the purposes of this list, *business* is defined as an enterprise that has been reported by an owner or known by an owner's family, relatives, clients, or Allen Subdivision neighbors as operating for profit, whether publicly listed or not. It is significant to note that, while some residents operated their businesses full or part-time from commercial buildings or sites, others utilized their skills and trades, equipment, vehicles, and rooms or personal space to conduct business in their homes as a means to supplement family income.

5

Education: From Limited to Open Access

The schooling of Allen's youth and other racial and ethnic minorities in Tallahassee included multiple layers of constraints. Up to 1963, the dual system of public education separated children by race. Segregation in the Leon County School System dictated limited schools that Black students could attend. Prior to this time, Black youth were assigned to all-Black schools, according to their home addresses in the county. In these schools, equipment and facilities were substandard and Black children studied with used, torn, and marked-up books handed down from other district schools. In addition, Blacks were not allowed to apply their intellectual skills or physical agility against their White counterparts in spelling bees, oratorical contests, or sports.

During the 1958–59 school year, one of Allen's own, Deloris Mills Massey Harpool, (the author), placed second among sixth-grade competitors in the entire Leon County School District spelling bee. Looking back on the experience, I shared,

> After growing up, I often wondered what it would have been like for me
> to compete against students in all-White schools. That opportunity was just
> not there. My prize was a Polaroid camera, and I was grateful and ecstatic
> to get it! But sometimes, looking back, I wonder if the prizes for first,
> second and third-place district-wide winners were the same for students in
> all-Black schools as they were for students in all-White schools.

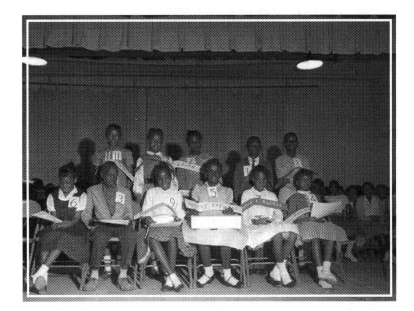

Black Sixth Grade Spelling Bee finalists (1960). Seated among other contestants on the front row are: Dorothy Caswell (#5)- winner, from Griffin Middle School; Deloris Mills (#9) – Second Place from Bond Elementary School and Annie L. Tucker (#7) – Third Place, from Raney Elementary School. Courtesy of the Tallahassee Democrat.

Very few children raised in Allen attended primary schools that were not on the south side of Tallahassee. Some 2014 survey respondents were born outside of Allen Subdivision, but they later relocated with their parents to the neighborhood. Two began their primary years in the late 1930s at the Wakulla County Shadeville Elementary School, and two began in the early 1940s in Tallahassee's Smokey Hollow community at St. John's Elementary School. Three other respondents began their late-1940s and mid-1950s primary schooling in Northwest (later renamed John G. Riley) Elementary School, Southwest (later renamed Pineview) Elementary School, and at a school in Pensacola, Florida, respectively.

Before the fall of 1959, children in Allen largely attended Bond or Lucy Moten Elementary and Middle Schools. Afterward, Robert Frank Nims School was opened as another middle school for African American children on Tallahassee's south side. At this time, the Leon County District School System offered Black children only two choices for high schools: the Original Lincoln High School or FAMU High School.

A series of events ignited mandatory changes in school choices for children born in the mid- to late 1950s in Allen and across Leon County. The changes were met with strong resistance by the school system, contributing to turbulent times in Tallahassee's education system. The late reverend C. K. Steele led a short boycott against the school system. Along with court challenges and federally required corrective actions, his leadership helped to bridge the divide. In 1954, the US Supreme Court had already ruled that the segregation of American schools by race was unconstitutional. Yet, according to the May 21, 2006 edition of the *Tallahassee Democrat*, as of 1956, "10 schools in Leon County continued to operate as black-only schools." These included four of the schools mentioned above where Allen children were mainly enrolled.

The landmark passage of the Civil Rights Act of 1964 did not appear to move Leon County's district school officials. They were slow to comply with the sweeping federal mandate. The *Democrat* further chronicled events that led to broader educational access and opportunity for new generations of Blacks in the county. Because of the district's continued discriminatory practices, parents took further action. The May 2006 article reported that, in March of 1962, Black parents filed a class-action suit in federal district court against the Leon County School Board. In February of 1963, the federal court ordered Leon County to submit a purposeful desegregation plan for more affirmative results. By September of the same year, the system saw minuscule changes. Only three Black teens had enrolled in Leon High School, and only one Black student had enrolled at Sullivan Elementary School.

The article further revealed that only two additional African American students were attending Leon High School by 1965. Alexander Henry, who grew up at 1302 Melvin Street, was one of the African Americans to enroll at Rickards High School in 1967. It was built on Tallahassee's south side in 1960. During the subsequent years, other Allen youth followed, as Rickards was the high school they were zoned to attend. Unfortunately, it took the Leon County School Board over fifteen years after the Supreme Court's ruling on school desegregation to develop an acceptable plan that, with modifications, was finally approved by the district court.

By 1970, Leon County schools were desegregated, and all-Black schools no longer existed in the county. This cleared the way for Allen youth born in the fifties, sixties, and later to attend other schools. Of this group, a small number of 2014 survey respondents who entered middle school in the mid- to late sixties and later reported having attended Raa and Fairview Middle Schools. Others continued to enroll at Nims and FAMU for middle school. From this point, in addition to reported enrollments in the Original Lincoln and FAMU High Schools, some Allen youth enrolled at Godby and Leon, but substantially more enrolled at Rickards High School.

The "Original" Lincoln High School was an all-Black school located in the Frenchtown area at 438 Brevard Street. It closed in 1967. In 1975, the local establishment built a new, predominately White school and assigned to it the same name, "Lincoln High School." The new school was to serve 9th through 12th grade students in a different area of Tallahassee at 3838 Trojan Trail. The term "Original" reflects the locally accepted means by which the first, Black Lincoln High School, is being honored in Tallahassee. The physical site of the Original Lincoln High School was converted for use as a community center, a library and a small museum featuring the history of the previous school.

For Allen's grade school students, in-home learning aides were scarce. At a minimum and when affordable, some families attained at least one dictionary and a set of encyclopedias. Electronic devices such as desk or laptop computers, mobile phones, Ipods, Ipads, Kindles, or printers were not available for the early Allen families. Up to at least the mid – to late 80s, students used the resources in the school library to complete research and other home work assignments.

College or vocational education was a must, as it was highly valued and conveyed by Allen parents. Of forty-one 2014 Allen survey participants, 90 percent indicated that they had received postsecondary education, including earning bachelors, masters, or doctoral degrees. Others received certifications in specialized skill areas, such as bookkeeping, auto mechanics, or general contracting. Varying resources funded education and training, including parents, part-time and full-time jobs, loans, scholarships, and grants. A few received help through the Servicemen's Readjustment Act of 1944, known as the GI Bill. For eligible, returning World War II veterans, this law provided benefits that included cash payments to cover tuition and living expenses for education in a university, high school, or vocational education center.

Most Allenites attended FAMU. Practically next door, it was familiar and more affordable than universities requiring out-of-town or out-of-state fees, lodging and travel. The entire college community offered loving, caring, relatable, receptive, and successful people who looked like Allenites; understood their needs; and showed genuine interest in their success before and after graduation. Each FAMU graduate can affirm a greater sense of pride, self-esteem, and clarity about who he or she is; hurdles overcome by his or her ancestors; his or her ability to compete in the world of work; and his or her unique value as a worthy contributor in society.

Our Help in Ages Past: The Churches in Allen

Allen Subdivision is primarily a Protestant community where Christian living, love of God and fellow people, and godly behavior were commonly taught. In its northern section, the community housed two churches: Gethsemane Missionary Baptist Church and St. Michael and All Saints Episcopal Church. These churches are credited with fostering early spiritual development for the inner strength needed in turbulent times, nurturing positive belief systems, promoting appropriate social behavior, helping to develop Christian leaders and providing Christian mentors for Allen's youth. Although different in style, organization, and member profile, both collectively provided social activities and civic support.

Gethsemane Missionary Baptist Church

Gethsemane Missionary Baptist Church. Image courtesy of Deloris Harpool

Historically, most of the residents of Allen attended Gethsemane Missionary Baptist Church. According to Gethsemane's written history, the church was founded in 1935, when its members separated from the mother Tabernacle Missionary Baptist Church. The newly formed congregation initially held services and conducted business in rented space. The pastor, Reverend W. M. Ming, led the organization with the support of C. S. Brazil, chairman of the deacon board.

In 1944, Reverend C. J. King, pastor, backed by Deacon Board Chairman F. Tolbert, spearheaded the first remodeling of a structure at 1301 Hudson Street. The church was again remodeled in 1965 under Reverend Sylvester R. Bright, FAMU professor of religion and philosophy. At this time, Reverend Bright led Gethsemane to become the local home church for scores of FAMU students. In the late 1960s, the college students filled the pews quickly, leaving standing room only at 11:00 a.m. services. The deacon and deaconess board members included Hattie Adams, Clifford Baulkman, C. S. Brazil, Nathaniel Charleston, E. G. Graham, Oma L. Homer, William Jefferson Sr., Samuel Mayo, Jesse Ware, and James White.

According to Allen residents, Gethsemane offered various meaningful benefits to its youth and adult members. In addition to helping them establish and maintain relationships with God, the church offered them the opportunity to learn Bible verses, songs, and hymns important for life. "Amazing Grace" was a hymn commonly sung in the church to nourish the soul. Its lyrics promoted spiritual strength and remembrance of the source of that strength. Particularly resonating for residents were the words, "Through many dangers, toils and snares, I have already come; 'tis grace that brought me safe thus far, and grace will lead me home."

Gethsemane also offered opportunities for children, college students, and young adults to receive leadership training through observation of church leaders. This experience helped youth to grasp the meaning of and develop the ability to sustain traditional religious practices of the church. Specific activities that were most meaningful to Allen residents were Sunday school, children's and collegiate choirs, prayer meetings, Bible study, the Baptist Training Union (BTU), choir unions, and Christmas and Easter plays and programs.

Young Melvin Beal on front lawn of Gethsemane Church. Image courtesy of Melvin Beal.

While some college students taught Sunday school and helped youth to prepare for Christmas and Easter programs, others joined the Gethsemane Gospel Choir and carried out other roles in the church. In the mid-1960s, the choir director, FAMU student Henry L. Porter, led the choir to become what was considered by many to be the "best church choir in town." Porter later became Bishop Dr. Henry L. Porter, leader of the Westcoast Center for Human Development in Sarasota, Florida. Marion J. Wade, another FAMU student, served as a Gethsemane assistant pastor in the 1960s. He later became Pastor of Perfecting the Saints Family Worship Center in Fayetteville, North Carolina.

Another FAMU student, and 1980s resident of Van Buren Street, was the late Frank Graham, a faithful church member who was elected president of the FAMU Student Government Association. He became the first student member of the Florida Board of Regents, the governing board of Florida's state universities. Other Allen youth became pastors or ministers, deacons, deaconesses, care leaders, wardens, missionary aides, and other officers and program leaders in churches throughout the United States.

In 1989, under Reverend Nathaniel Sumpter, the church laid the foundation for a new building at 302 Wallis Street in Tallahassee. The facility was completed in 1998 under Reverend Dossie Bivens. Church members occupied the new building in February 2000. Two years later, the True Fellowship Holiness Church congregation purchased the previous Gethsemane Church building on Hudson Street. The original church structure still stands at the corner of FAMU Way and Hudson Street, which was renamed True Fellowship Court.

One remnant left in the earlier Hudson Street building was the church bell. It had been mounted high in the church's tower. The relic rang out on Sunday mornings to signal the beginning of Sunday school. Allen residents report that church officials also rang the bell when neighborhood residents or church members passed away.

After the 2005 resignation of Reverend Bivens, Reverend Dock Roberts served as interim pastor for eighteen months. Reverend Dr. B. J. Virgil was selected as pastor on August 14, 2006. The recorded history of the church cites the service of other prior ministers since its 1935 founding. Reverend W. L. Webb, Reverend A. E. Isaacs, Reverend T. E. Gainous, Reverend Leroy Thomas, and Reverend William Boyd were among other pastors listed.

Elder George Proctor Jr. was selected as pastor on March 2, 2010. Under his leadership, the Wallis Street establishment saw rapid growth in its membership and ministries. The church underwent physical upgrades and renovations, including changes in the church sanctuary. As of 2015, the church body continued to include a sizable group of dedicated current and previous residents of Allen Subdivision.

St. Michael and All Angels Episcopal Church

St Michael and All Saints Episcopal Church after front entrance was relocated from Hudson Street to Melvin Street. Image courtesy of Rector, Hugh Chapman.

Under its unique governance structure, St. Michael and All Angels Episcopal Church ultimately became a supportive establishment for FAMU students, Allen youth, and other parishioners. The first leader of the church was Jacob R. Ballard who, in 1882, was the second Black deacon ordained in the Episcopal Church, Diocese of Florida.

According to the written history of the church, in 1888, Bishop E. W. Weed gave the church a new facility for services. He also changed the name of the church to St. Michael and All Angels Episcopal Church. FAMU President D. T. Tucker, the first lay reader of the church, assisted Rector W. H. Carter, the Priest-in-Charge, in establishing regular services and Sunday school. A parochial school established under the church authority served at least two students, among whom community leaders emerged. For over the first sixty years after the church received its new building, multiple priests from Tallahassee area churches assisted in leading the congregation. Reverend Dr. W. H. Carter of Tallahassee's St. John's Episcopal Church was one among those who served. By 2017, Reverend Hugh Chapman was appointed as church rector.

The development and growth of the church are significant in the history of and contributions to the Allen neighborhood. By 1947, Father David Henry Brooks, Episcopal chaplain at FAMU, became the first long-term leader of St. Michael. Among his notable achievements, Brooks led the increase in membership, including students from across the United States and abroad. During the Civil Rights Movement, he assisted students and activists in conducting strategy meetings for nonviolent protest marches in downtown Tallahassee. He also prepared students for confirmation by the Diocesan Bishop and developed the Canterbury Club for college students.

Father David Henry Brooks, former Rector of St. Michael and All Angels Episcopal Church

With further vision, Father Brooks influenced the building of a chapel, the Parish Canterbury House, at 1405 Melvin Street. Before the chapel was erected, the main entrance to the church was on Hudson Street. Known to locals as the Parish House, the chapel became a popular site for teenage dances and group performances. Sponsored in the early to mid-1960s, the Friday and Saturday night events were the first known by Allen youth to be held in a church facility.

According to former state senator Alfred Lawson, current member of the US House of Representatives and long-time member of St. Michael, the church leadership supported Father Brooks in providing teenage dances. However, the church leadership did not want to sponsor dances on the Fridays or Saturdays when local football games were held. It would be too late in the evenings to start dances after football games. Therefore, according to Representative Lawson, "dances were held at the Parish House on Friday and Saturday nights when no high school football games were held."

In spite of church outreach efforts, few Allen residents attended or joined St. Michael. The membership primarily comprised professionals from other Tallahassee communities. Although most Allenites were oriented to or reared in the Baptist tradition, Father Brooks continued his outreach mission. As a result, he became a compassionate mentor to Allen youth and others throughout the city. He continued to authorize and supervise street parties for children in his church and in Allen. His love for people and children was well recognized by people throughout and external to Tallahassee and the state. According to the church history, St. Michael's congregation honored Brooks in April of 1995 as they rededicated the Parish Hall and renamed it "The David Henry Brooks Hall."

St. Michael's offerings were diverse. The church hosted weekly Sunday services and communion, postservice fellowship, Bible study, Sunday school, and choirs with guest artists from FAMU and Florida State University (FSU). Traditionally, children served as acolytes and lay Eucharistic ministers. They assisted with communion, served as lay readers, and assisted with the scripture in Sunday services. Extracurricular activities were available at the church for youth and college students. Over the years, trainees became junior and senior wardens and members of the vestry. Many have claimed leadership roles in and outside the local church and Florida.

St. Michael and All Angels Episcopal Church Acolytes and Father David Brooks,
1956. Left to right: Kirk Simpson, Anthony Foster, Father Brooks, Henry M. Brooks
and Bishop Holifield. Photo courtesy of church archivist, Alexis R. McMillan.

Integral Relationship with Florida A&M University

The relocation of the State Normal College for Colored Students (later Florida A&M University) from its original Copeland Street site sparked new opportunities for African Americans on the south side of Tallahassee. With its 1891 funding under the Morrill Act, the college became the first land-grant institution for Black people in Florida. This designation would draw additional African American students to its campus. In addition, by the early 1900s, it became a magnet for potential employees and builders as it broadened employment opportunities and its community service population south of the Tallahassee Seaboard Coastline (CSX) railroad tracks.

As the college expanded to become Florida Agricultural and Mechanical University (FAMU), many benefits accrued to individuals settling in its vicinity, including affordable housing. Allen Subdivision residents took advantage of its offerings in education, employment, health, social, and cultural enrichment, entertainment, athletics, and sports. They received formal education, training, and services through varying academic units and programs. Some adults enrolled in FAMU's 1960s Trade and Technical Education Programs. Youth in Allen enrolled in the University's Lucy Moten Elementary and Middle School and in the FAMU High School, later renamed FAMU Developmental Research School (DRS). Over subsequent years, Allen residents received baccalaureate, masters, and doctoral degrees at FAMU.

Lucy Moten School Building on the campus of Florida A&M University, where many Allen youth attended grade school. Image courtesy of Deloris Harpool.

In the employment arena, the university provided jobs for Allen residents. Their positions ranged from domestic workers to chief executives. Some residents were hired as elementary, high school, and college faculty, staff, and administrators. Others served as maintenance and grounds keepers, dormitory housekeepers, campus laundry employees, and dining facility staff. Once enrolled, teens and young adults secured jobs on campus as student assistants in clerical and other support positions at the university.

Individuals who participated in the 2014 Allen Subdivision survey cited multiple benefits of living or growing up near the university. Frequently noted by survey respondents, FAMU was an entertainment mecca where residents received cultural enrichment and opportunities to appreciate the performing arts in FAMU's Charles Winterwood Theater, Lee Hall and Perry Paige Auditoriums. They noted art exhibits, concerts, speech competitions, and theatrical productions as events remembered from childhood to present-day offerings. Some informants reported that their first experiences with opera singers, symphony orchestra performances, world famous lecturers, and modern dance performers took place on the campus of Florida A&M University. Productions by the FAMU Children's Theater, led by Dr. Irene Edmunds, were also noted among the expressed memoirs of some Allen residents.

Survey respondents further reported social and athletic events. Attending Friday night movies at FAMU's Lee Hall was among the social experiences noted. College football games in FAMU's Bragg Stadium; basketball games in the Jake Gaither Gymnasium; and track and field events were among other perks residents cited. Informants frequently listed homecoming parades, featuring the world-famous Marching 100 Band, among memories about FAMU.

The Allen community frequently used the physical grounds of the university for more than school-related activities. Allen's youth played softball, baseball, football, kickball, dodgeball, and volleyball and performed acrobatics on the university's recreational fields. One field was conveniently located at the corner of Boulevard Street (Martin Luther King Boulevard) and Canal Street (FAMU Way). It was directly across the street from the western boundary of the College View Subdivision. At the west end of West Harrison Street, under a small, covered FAMU pavilion, the City's recreation department sponsored programs, where Allen youth gathered for summer arts and crafts, recreation, and snacks.

At the corner of South Bronough Street and Palmer Avenue, FAMU's Gibbs Park was another site where Allen youth played. This open-access park offered rolling hills; well-padded, plush green grass; and wide-open space for play. The park featured a large concrete platform used to stage outdoor presentations and May Day activities. May Day spectators looked forward to the annual ritual when children would plait the May Pole. Children from Allen took full advantage of the concrete stage to produce make-believe shows, roller skate, ride bicycles, play board games, and engage in acrobatics and other wholesome activities. When the park closed, the vacant lot became the site of the current FAMU Allied Health and Nursing Complex.

Between 1926 and 1971, the Florida A&M University Hospital gave medical care to Allen residents and others within the Tallahassee vicinity. Although some infants in Allen were born at home with the assistance of midwives, the FAMU Hospital was the birthing place for others. Located adjacent to and directly south of Allen Subdivision, the hospital was an obvious perk.

Professional African American role models for Allen youth naturally came with the FAMU package, igniting career aspiration and enhanced social skills among youth in the neighborhood. Allen residents were directly exposed to individuals operating and leading a successful, nationally renowned university. Through these individuals, Allen youth and adults observed and interacted with African Americans who looked like them and whose early socioeconomic backgrounds were similar to theirs. In addition to executive leaders and teachers, FAMU produced famous athletes and other college students and alumni that Allen residents knew and grew to admire.

At the same time, Allen provided valuable support to FAMU. African American vendors in the neighborhood served university students, faculty, and employees in multiple ways. Among the types of venues available were grocery stores, a jewelry repair shop, a radio repair shop, a butcher, cleaners, an upholstery shop, taxi services, child care, beauty and barbershops, seamstresses, a service station, a fish market, café/restaurants, clubs and boarding houses. "Allen families also provided in-home laundering and ironing services to support FAMU employees and students.

Allenites opened their homes in significant numbers to accommodate the residential needs of FAMU constituents. Among other boarding houses, the home of the parents of the late congresswoman Carrie Pittman Meek was a well-known site in the community. It housed FAMU women who were not able to attain dormitory rooms or who chose not to live on the college campus. Commonly known as the Pittman Boarding House, this demolished structure once stood a block north of the campus, at the corner of South Bronough Street and Jennings (currently Jakes and Patterson) Street. Both male and female students found housing in the neighborhood.

Sonya Nunn Seay, a 1973 FAMU computer science graduate, lived three doors down the street from the Pittman Boarding House. According to Seay, not all students who lived in boarding houses did so because they could not attain dormitory space on campus: "The arrangements were made for me to stay with the Jeffersons. I was not given a choice to live in the dormitory. I am not so sure if I was given a choice I would have chosen to live in the dormitory. Living with the Jeffersons was like living at home."

In addition, through Gethsemane Missionary Baptist Church and St. Michael and All Saints Episcopal Church, Allen Subdivision addressed the spiritual needs of FAMU employees and students. Both of these establishments allowed students to play active roles and develop strong leadership skills needed in church, social, and civic leadership positions. In addition, they supported students in unique ways during the students' fight for civil rights.

Involvement in the Civil Rights Movement

During the mid-1950s and the 1960s, Allen Subdivision uniquely hosted notable events in the Tallahassee's Civil Rights Movement. The role of the community took on specific importance in 1956, when FAMU student activists Wilhelmina Jakes and Carrie Patterson were subjected to racial discrimination on a city bus. During their residency in an Allen Subdivision boarding house at 123 Jennings Street, they had refused to move to the back of a city bus and were arrested for their act of defiance. The brave young women garnered support from local activists and FAMU students to launch the 1956 Tallahassee bus boycott. It also prompted a march in protest to the discriminatory practices the women had experienced.

Consequently, a cross was burned in the front yard of their Jennings Street home. This dreadful act, the first ever witnessed in Allen Subdivision, was thought to have been committed by individuals resisting the victims' fight for civil rights. Susie Brown, long-term resident at 127 West Jennings Street, witnessed the cross burning that prompted the Tallahassee bus boycott. She confirmed that, at the time of this violent and intimidating event, Wilhelmina and Carrie were renting a room from her next-door neighbors, the Kendricks. She stated, "I personally saw the cross burning in their front yard next door to my house."

When the Tallahassee bus boycotts, marches, and sit-ins were launched, Allen Subdivision became a primary connector for college students and activists as they made their way from FAMU's campus. The protesters traveled north through the neighborhood down Hudson,

Melvin, Bronough, and Boulevard Streets. They turned east onto Canal Street (FAMU Way) and north onto Adams Street to reach the downtown commercial district.

Students and NAACP activists march past Gethsemane Church, as they travel to a downtown staging site for their non-violent protest against racial discrimination. (1960s) Image courtesy of Tallahassee Democrat.

Gethsemane Missionary Baptist Church and St. Michael and All Saints Episcopal Church were neighborhood sites that offered relief and support to student civil rights protesters. Gethsemane became a refuge for protesters who were forced from downtown into Allen by law enforcement officers. It provided local shelter and water for students to wash tear gas from their eyes. At St. Michael and All Saints Episcopal Church on Melvin Street, Father David Brooks hosted organizational meetings to help activists prepare for nonviolent protests prior to their marches.

Allen residents observed the marches in awe from their front porches and yards. Some residents, including Mable Allison Webster and her sister, Earlene Allison Farmer, previous Hudson Street residents, participated in the protests. They reported witnessing the violent reaction of law enforcement officers who met the protesters with harsh force. Earlene stated, "The police forced us back into Allen Subdivision with water hoses and tear gas. I ran with the college students into Gethsemane Church. They threw tear gas into the church to flush us out. We were arrested, fingerprinted, and held in the fenced back yard of the county jail on Gaines Street until someone from FAMU bailed us out."

Nostalgic Sounds of Allen

Multiple factors created a combination of sounds unique to Allen Subdivision from the mid-1930s through the mid-1970s. The factors included the topography; housing and lifestyle; proximity to railroad tracks; and the presence of churches, clubs, FAMU, and FAMU's public hospital. Collectively, the sounds were spiritually uplifting, entertaining, comforting, amusing, and sometimes alarming.

On Sunday mornings, the harmonious sounds of the gospel choir and traditional hymns bellowed through the open wood-frame windows of Gethsemane Missionary Baptist Church. These sounds created a sense of well-being in the neighborhood. A large rusty bell mounted in the church steeple alerted the community to the opening of Sunday school. Church officials also rang the bell to notify the community of the death of a church member or Allen resident. During Sunday worship services and in weekly prayer meetings, an indescribable peace filled the air when the church elders lined hymns, sang and moaned in perfect harmony. They said that when they moaned, God could hear their souls' cry, even if they "never said a mumbling word."

The sound of pounding rain on tin roofs in the neighborhood was a welcomed elixir. The daily awakening sound of roosters crowing across the community pleasantly signaled the beginning of a new day. The peaceful sound of clear, shallow water trickling through the canal between West Van Buren and Canal Streets was a pleasant treat, as children cooled their feet in the flowing water or walked and scooted on the two large pipes spanning the canal.

During the fall, before the 1970s, the rhythmic sounds of the FAMU Marching 100 Band from its practice field provided daily entertainment. Aspiring FAMU music students unknowingly favored the community as they practiced musical runs on string, woodwind, brass, and percussion instruments throughout the day. They practiced and studied in wood-frame barracks previously located at the top of South Bronough Street behind FAMU's Lee Hall Auditorium. After the barracks were demolished, these sounds were confined to the new band hall constructed in the center of the campus.

Rhythm and blues selections blasted over the walls of the Peppermint Patio on Canal Street. During weekends and on weeknights, these sounds prompted some Allen residents and teens to dance in their yards. Other residents reported covering their ears for a peaceful night's sleep.

After the north–south streets were paved, rumbling roller skates and go-carts signaled races for adolescents and teens on Allen's inclines. Joyful screams of children's excitement while playing softball, kickball, dodgeball, and basketball in the streets or in open fields created good feelings for the entire neighborhood. Residents were tickled when hearty laughter erupted in small groups as teens and young adults "played the dozens" or "signified on each other."

Some sounds, however, were quite common and frightening. Deafening sirens alarmed residents when Strong and Jones Funeral Home ambulances raced patients up Hudson Street to the FAMU Hospital. On the northern edge of the community, loud whistles, squealing iron wheels, and thunderous rumblings alerted area residents as east–west Seaboard Coastline passenger and CSX freight trains passed through the neighborhood.

10

A Fading Family Residential Community

In spite of the occasional sound of ambulances and trains passing through, Allen Subdivision has been known as a pleasant, quiet residential community. However, multiple forces brought about a reduction in the number of families living within its borders. As of 1960, at least 205 families lived in the community. Since this period, some homes have been sacrificed via eminent domain to make way for city, county, or state plans.

In 1985, the Florida Legislature approved construction of the M. S. Thomas Bridge that passes over Canal Street (FAMU Way) at the northeast edge of the neighborhood. From the north, this four-lane Duval/Bronough Street overpass supplanted a part of Hudson Street as it merged onto South Adams Street at the intersect of Harrison Street. The bridge required the removal or demolition of establishments and homes along West Van Buren, Canal (FAMU Way), West Harrison, Hudson, and Melvin Streets. The project affected home and business owners in significant proportions, as they were displaced and forced to sell their properties.

White home at corner of Canal and Hudson Streets prior to FAMU Way Project changes (Top Image) and Lawrence family home (Middle and Lower Images) hoisted for relocation from Canal Street (FAMU Way), directly adjacent to original site of several demolished Black-owned businesses (1983). Image courtesy of Cherry Lawrence.

By the early 1990s, other changes occurred after FAMU purchased property in the northwestern section of the neighborhood. The university's purchase would accommodate a new building and parking space for its School of Pharmacy. The new structure occupied parcels on West Pershing Street, South Bronough, West Harrison, and South Boulevard Streets.

Some of the dwellings that owners were forced to sell were homes that dually served as business sites. Mattie Mobley, a previous resident, remembers the period when area changes affected her life in Allen. She had operated a beauty salon and a boarding house in her home before it was demolished. "I had to move out of my home on West Harrison Street in 1989," said Mobley.

In the immediate vicinity, on South Bronough Street, other homeowners had vacated their property before their parcels of land became a FAMU administrative office site. A two-story wood-frame structure designated as FAMU's Booster Office was built at the site on the 1300 block of South Bronough Street, north of Harrison Street. Still other residents and owners relocated before student apartments were built on the same block and on the same street.

Some residents were relocated to other parts of Tallahassee before the Anita Favors Plaza was constructed where businesses and homes once existed west of Adams Street and east of Railroad Avenue (Wahnish Way). Demolitions included structures that had previously existed in the 100 and 200 blocks of Canal Street (FAMU Way), the 200 and 300 blocks of West Van Buren Street, and the 1200 block of South Bronough Street. Apartments, with parking beneath each unit, replaced duplexes in the Taylor development, where twenty-eight families had previously lived. The Taylor development was located at the corner of Martin Luther King Boulevard and West Van Buren Street. Observation of these changes prompted residents' concerns about how FAMU's expansion and city redevelopment plans might affect their homes in the neighborhood.

The Leon County Board of County Commissioners and the Tallahassee City Commission's Blueprint Intergovernmental Agency invested more than $1.5 million in physical enhancements that affected neighborhoods across Leon County. The agency's Capital Cascade Trail and FAMU Way Extension Project called for the redevelopment and extension of Canal Street (currently, FAMU Way). This undertaking required the purchase and demolition of additional homes and establishments in the northern segment of Allen Subdivision.

Prior to redevelopment affecting Allen Subdivision and other areas along FAMU Way, the Blueprint Intergovernmental Agency utilized community engagement among other methods to identify multiple issues that plagued the area. Problems identified included a dangerous ditch or canal that was twenty feet deep in some areas; flooding beneath the bridge over Monroe Street; narrow sidewalks; lack of adequate lighting, safety, and an outdoor pathway for walking along a street singularly used for vehicles; and the need for an additional connector to downtown, from Monroe Street to areas west of Wahnish Way.

According to the agency, when completed, the FAMU Way Extension Project would "provide an improved, safer roadway and enhanced mobility in the southern region" of Tallahassee, with "new benefits and recreational opportunities for the entire community."

Another factor that partially influenced the decrease in family residential dwellings is the upward mobility of the children of the original Allen residents. As of 2015, a few residents were still living in their original homes, although their offspring had acquired greater educational, employment, and housing opportunities. With these opportunities and the ability to make greater financial investments than their parents were afforded, children and grandchildren of the early residents purchased or moved into homes outside of the neighborhood, the city, and the state. Some of their surviving parents also relocated to other areas of Tallahassee or to other cities. Some of the heirs to homes in Allen converted their dwellings to student housing units for rental income. Students became chief occupants of duplexes, apartments, and homes in the area.

11

Successes of Early Sons and Daughters of Allen

Congresswoman Carrie Pittman Meek (right) during a moment of sharing and celebration with Leon County Commissioner, William Proctor, Jr. (left) in the early 2000s.

In spite of its humble beginnings, widespread discrimination, and long-term economic challenges, Allen Subdivision has produced amazing results among its residents and their children. Listed below are thirty-one 2015 "Super Significant Senior" honorees from the early Allen family, their brief biographies, and comments regarding their days in Allen. The average age of the honorees is ninety-one. The age shown for each honoree is the age reported when his or her information was verified by telephone and recorded by

Queen Bruton, Cherry Lawrence, and Deloris Harpool. Although some of the honorees made their heavenly transitions prior to the publishing of this document, their legacies still live on.

Irene Allen, 101, (deceased) was educated in Wakulla County, Florida. She lived in the 1400 block of Hudson Street in Allen Subdivision from 1952 to 1964. Irene raised seven children: Barbara, Jonnie Mae, Remus (deceased), Jerrlyne, Clytia (deceased), Gloria, and Jerry (deceased).) She worked in the home of one of the owners of the Mendelson's Department Store of downtown Tallahassee and the Northwood Mall, retiring after fifty-two years of work. Her great memory of Allen was that it was a very close-knit and family-oriented community.

James R. ("R.C.") Anderson, 85, (deceased) lived in Allen Subdivision from 1929 to 1955 on Van Buren Street and on Melvin Street. He attended the Original Lincoln High School and enrolled in FAMC for one year before it became a university. James earned a BS degree in industrial education at FAMU and certification in supervision and administration at Nova University. He spent two years in the army and married Aretha Fields Anderson. They had four children: LaCrecha, Andrea, James Jr., and Quentin. R. C. remembered Allen Subdivision as "a closely knitted community where people enjoyed each other like brothers and sisters." He also expressed special memories of his time spent in the Allen neighborhood playing with the champion Hillside Sluggers Softball Team.

Leroy Baker, 81, lived on five streets in Allen Subdivision, including South Boulevard (Martin Luther King Boulevard), South Bronough, Pershing, Hudson, and Van Buren Streets. He and his family moved out of the neighborhood in 1962. Leroy and his wife, Johnnie, raised two children: John and Carol. At FAMU, Baker majored in mathematics. In 1965, he received a bachelor of arts degree in vocational education. As a senior vocational instructor, he taught electronics engineering technology and retired after thirty-four years of teaching. He reported holding memories of living very close to FAMU and enjoying the various activities sponsored on campus and the many benefits offered his children in the university's elementary and high schools.

Rosa T. Brown, 80, as a member of the Allen Subdivision extended family, spent many hours in the neighborhood with her sister, Oma L. Homer, and her mother-in-law, Loujetta Brown. She married Loujetta's son, Wilbert Brown, and bore twin girls, Harriet and Clarriet. Rosa completed her master of education degree at FAMU and a specialist degree in counseling and human systems at FSU. She is a member of the Alpha Upsilon Zeta Chapter of Zeta Phi Beta Sorority Inc. and has held numerous local, state, and national positions in the sorority. She received multiple awards for her leadership and service at all levels. She was the executive director and founder of the Zeta Educational Thespian Association and founder of the Mosely House Museum in Eatonville, Florida. Brown retired from the position of director of guidance and counseling with the Leon County School District after many years of administrative and teaching services.

Susie Brown, 85, has been a resident of Allen for over fifty years. She graduated from FAMU High School and went into private business as a seamstress. She and her husband, Hubert Brown Sr., raised six children on Jennings (renamed Jakes and Patterson) Street. Their children are Gwendolyn, LaJoyce, Judith, Hubert Jr. (deceased), Wayne (deceased), and Hortense. "Sue" was Sunday school secretary and currently serves as a deaconess at Gethsemane Missionary Baptist Church. She also was a member of the Capital City Democratic Women's Club. She witnessed the cross burning in Allen on Jennings Street that was associated with the 1956 bus boycott. "Ms. Sue," as she is called, shared her fond memories of "the quietness of the neighborhood and enjoying the way the Allen kids bonded and supported one another."

Queen Bruton, 83, (deceased) enjoyed nine to ten years in Allen Subdivision. She and her husband, George, raised four children: Angela, Sharon, Everett, and Colleen. Queen earned a bachelor of arts degree from FAMU and taught in Broward, Wakulla, and Duval County schools for thirty-two years, collectively. She received prestigious awards for her community service. Her memberships in church, political, social, service, civic, and professional organizations continued until her health declined. She shared "memories of years spent in Allen, including playing in the streets, walking on pipes between Canal and Van Buren Streets, and attending numerous activities at FAMC." She also shared that some cherished moments were her days in Sunday school and her days in the Girl Scouts at Lucy Moten, under the direction of Eloise Wright.

Hattie Ruth Dennis, 81, lived on West Van Buren Street. She married Joseph Dennis, and together they had eight children: Karen Jones Gillespie, Faye Jones Johnson, Kenneth Jones, Sheila Dennis (deceased), Karla Dennis Bragg, Cassandra Dennis Ramirez, Dr. Alfred D. Dennis, and Eric Shields. She graduated from FAMU with a bachelor's degree in English and a master's degree in guidance and counseling. Her career included teaching in Wakulla County at Cobb Junior High, serving as a teacher and counselor at Nims Middle School, being the counselor and coordinator for the Lively Vocational Center CETA Program, and working as a district-wide hospital home-bound instructor. She retired from her employment with the Leon County School Board after thirty-five years in education. Hattie remembers "Allen Subdivision as a close-knit community, where everyone cared about each other."

Alton Farmer, 81, resided in Allen Subdivision from 1957 to 1985. With his first and second wives, he became the father of seven children: Phaedra, Hiram, Ivan, Duane, Cassandra, Anthony, and Jarvis. He attained a bachelor of science degree at FAMU in 1955 in the field of health and physical education. In his early years after college, Farmer was a teacher at Stevens Elementary School in Quincy, Florida. He worked for thirty-three years, collectively, as a middle school teacher in the Leon County School District and in the Imperial Unified School District of Imperial, California. Farmer remembered Allen Subdivision "as a close-knit residential community" and fondly recalled "the friendliness of the people."

Pinkie Felder, 84, (deceased) was born at 1422 South Bronough Street. She married Lorenzo Felder Sr. and became the mother of four children: Barbara, Sylvia, Monica, and Lorenzo Jr. She also raised her grandson, Derrick. Her family was among the first homeowners in the community when their home was built in 1928. She was delivered at home by Georgia Long, an Allen resident and local midwife. Felder's memories of Allen included "playing spring board" and Sally Go Round the Moon. She remembered that her brother, Dahwee, built wagons that they rode up and down the Bronough Street hill. She also shared that her first doll was made of grass.

Geneva Clack Ferguson, 81, was the youngest of five children and was born on Van Buren Street. She was delivered by Allen's famous midwife, Georgia Long. Her family later moved to the corner of Canal and Hudson Streets, where she lived until her graduation from FAMU with a bachelor of science degree. She attended the Original Lincoln High School. For fifty years, Geneva was married to H. Lionel Ferguson. She was the mother of two children, Lynette and Juanda Genice. She was an elementary school teacher for thirty-five years and served the Dade County School Board for eight years as a reading specialist. She joined the United Teachers of Dade County and was awarded Teacher of the Year.

Easter Ferrell, 80+, (deceased) moved to Allen Subdivision from Quincy, Florida, in 1956. She lived on Van Buren Street before moving in 1962 to her home on Hudson Street. She married William Ferrell (deceased) and was employed as a waitress for thirty years at Ma Mary's Kitchen, which was owned by Mary Lamb (deceased), also a long-time resident of Allen Subdivision. Ferrell ran her own business, the Blue Ribbon café, on Canal Street for eleven years. A special memory for her was knowing Ben Washington, who ran a small grocery store on Melvin Street and who ran the Blue Ribbon Café before she took over management of the business. Her father worked on the railroad.

Mary Henry, 86, (deceased) was married to Alexander Henry and was the mother of seven children: Raymond Alan, Ronald Eugene, Alexander Jr., Kelvin Bernard (deceased), Hayward Charles, Lori Michelle, and Michael Curtis (deceased). Mrs. Henry lived in Allen Subdivision from 1948 to 1978. She attended Lucy E. Moten Elementary School and the Original Lincoln High School. She worked in the FAMU dining room for twenty-one years. Henry was a long-time member of Bethel Baptist Church and an avid bowler. As she reported, her proudest moments were watching her children grow up in Allen. She enjoyed making and selling delicious snow cones to neighborhood children. They were made with a special syrup and then topped with pineapple and condensed milk, as created by her mother-in-law, Leamus Henry.

Millie Inez Hicks, 88, (deceased) lived in the 1300 block of Melvin Street. She attended Lucy E. Moten Elementary School and Lincoln High School. Along with her mother, Annie Mae Long, Hicks raised five children: James, Adolph, Alvin, Annarene, and Gwendolyn. Hicks was employed at the FAMU dining hall and at the Florida State University dining hall for women. She also served as a domestic worker in a private home. As a seasoned senior, she lived from time to time in her residence in Allen and sometimes in Palm Harbor, Florida. What she often expressed about Allen is that the "families were and still are very close-knit. All families were and still are a true, united front—we still are a united community of one."

Carrie Belle Hoffman, 90, moved to Allen in 1943 to attend FAMU, where she was selected as Miss FAMC. This great-granddaughter of a Seminole Indian married Alphonso Ralph Hoffman Sr. and is the mother of Ralph (deceased), Marion, Ernest, Norma (deceased), Alphonso Jr., and Denise. She and her husband built the Ship Ahoy Restaurant and a residence on the corner of South Adams Street and Palmer Avenue. She says that in the early times, "Monroe Street was a dirt road and it did not come as far as Palmer Avenue." The property she and her husband bought from her uncle, Albert Crump, "was a cow pasture." Hoffman recalled the story of the Florida governor's car traveling up a clay road, Palmer Avenue, after a big rain to get to FAMU. His car slid into the ditch. She added, "Mr. Crump helped to get the governor's car out of the ditch, and that kind act caused the governor to join and lead the drive to get streets paved in Allen Subdivision."

Ruth Jackson, 89, (deceased) lived on Van Buren and Boulevard Streets and was in the Allen neighborhood for fifty-six years. She was the mother of six children: Leon Morris (deceased), Sarah Morris (deceased), Rev. Charles Morris, Rev. Shirley Greenwood, Rev. G. L. Jackson, and Douglas Morris. She attended FAMC in 1944 and worked as a clerk for the FAMU Housing Department. An active member of Bethel African Methodist Episcopal (AME) Church for seventy-two years, she served on several boards and participated in many ministries. "Eating at AD's Café and shopping at DuPont's Meat Market and Carroll's Ice House" were among her special memories. Ruth also expressed fond memories of walking across the canal pipes to Van Buren Street. In addition, she said "everybody knew and supported each other in the neighborhood."

Dennis Jefferson, 81, the youngest son of Richard and Eva Jefferson, attended Bond Elementary, Lucy E. Moten Elementary, FAMU High School, and FAMU. He was a star quarterback on his high school football team and played under the legendary Coach Jake Gaither while in college. He coached at Florida A&M, Mississippi Valley, and Shaw Universities. Dennis led two undefeated teams, was declared most outstanding player at the Orange Blossom Classic in 1957, and was voted coach of the year for two years by the Central Florida Athletic Conference. His fondest moment was when his alma mater inducted him into the FAMU Athletic Hall of Fame.

John Jefferson, 82, (deceased) was another son of Richard and Eva Jefferson. He lived in Allen from birth through most of his life, until the family house was sold to FAMU. The Pharmacy Building now sits on the former site of the home. He attended the Original Lincoln High School, where he was known as a talented athlete. John had a satisfying career in building construction and maintenance while living in Tallahassee and in Tampa. He recalled "helping to push cars out of the ditch on South Bronough Street."

William Jefferson Sr., 92, (deceased) was the oldest living son born to Richard and Eva Jefferson. William married Leola Jefferson (deceased) and had four children: Nancy,

William Jr., Paula, and Richard. William Sr. attended the Original Lincoln High School and worked over fifty years for the Capital City Country Club. Among others, he attended Trinity Missionary Baptist Church and served as a deacon. He added four bedrooms to his original house in order to accommodate FAMU students who needed housing near the campus. He loved to play golf and enjoyed raising his kids and watching his family grow up in the Allen neighborhood. He believed in keeping the neighborhood's special bond between neighbors and extended family.

James Cullen "JC" Lawrence, 83, lived at 130 Canal Street from 1939 until he earned a bachelor of science degree from FAMU. He married Betty Strong (deceased), and together, they raised three children: Mamie Johnson, daughter; Dale Fuller, daughter; and Darrel Lawrence, son. As a long-time member of Bethel Baptist Church, he served as chairman of the Deacon Board. After his military service, Lawrence served as "Negro Recreation Supervisor" for the City of Tallahassee, a position in which he directed activities such as roller skating, board games, and sports for Black teenagers in Tallahassee. Before retiring from that position, he also served as manager of the Jake Gaither Golf Course. Lawrence remembers receiving his master's degree, his years spent with family—especially being with his six grandchildren—and "playing ball" in his youth "with neighborhood friends in the empty lot where Saint Michael's Church is now located."

Rosco Long, 80+, brother of Virginia Pinkney, was raised by Benjamin J. and Georgia Long. He lived in Allen Subdivision and attended Lucy E. Moten Elementary School. He graduated from the Original Lincoln High School, where he was an avid football player. After high school, Long began a twenty-two-year career in the US Army. He lives in Columbus, Georgia, and retired from Fort Benning, Georgia. During his marriage to his loving wife Mary, he fathered two daughters. His uncle owned Bill's (Mr. Sip's) Fish Market, a neighborhood favorite in Allen, which Long's father took over after his uncle's death.

Samuel Long, 84, (deceased) lived in Allen with his grandparents, Benjamin J. and Georgia Long. He attended Lucy E. Moten Elementary School, FAMU High School, and the Original Lincoln High School, where he was a star football player. Samuel married his high school sweetheart, Connie (deceased), and was the father of one son, Samuel Jr. After his service in the US military, he returned to Tallahassee and earned his high school-equivalency diploma (GED). He worked in the FAMU Heating and Air Conditioning Department until his retirement in April of 1993 after thirty-five years with the university.

He was honored to be the driver to pull the float for Miss FAMU, the homecoming queen, and the homecoming court for over twenty-five years. He was a member of Saint Paul AME Church, where he served as deacon and member of the trustee and usher boards. He often said that he "loved being in the Alley."

Celia M. Matthews, 83, (deceased) was the daughter of Nellie and Robert Matthews. She grew up in Allen and attended FAMU High School. She is the mother of one daughter, Cecelia, and sister of James Matthews ("Pee Whiskey," deceased), a South Florida attorney. Celia worked for twenty-three years at a fraternity house at FSU and was a cook for forty years. She enjoyed serving during summer months as chef in prominent establishments in Atlantic City and Wildwood, New Jersey. She remembers how the "people of Allen stuck together in the neighborhood." She believed that "it takes a village to raise a child."

Carrie Pittman Meek, 88, (deceased) grew up in Allen Subdivision, and in early adulthood she lived with her parents at 1447 South Bronough Street, where they operated a boarding house for college women. Her father was a Georgia sharecropper and her grandfather was a slave. While living in Allen, Meek received a BS degree from FAMU and a master's degree from the University of Michigan. In Miami, her last residence, she and her husband, Harold H. Meek, raised three children: Luciagail Davis Rayford, Sheila Davis Kinui and Kendrick Meek. She taught at Bethune Cookman University and became an educational administrator. Among other leadership roles, she was a consultant and served on a health-service board. She served in the Florida House of Representatives from 1978 to 1983, after which she became a state senator. She was later elected to serve in the US Congress, a post in which she served until she retired. Affectionately known in Tallahassee as "Tot," Meek remembers growing up in Allen Subdivision near FAMU and being able to attend college near her own neighborhood.

Mary Governor Meeks, 83, (deceased) grew up in the 1300 block of South Bronough Street. She received the bachelor of science degree in education in 1954. Mary completed her master's degree in 1974, with an emphasis in library science. She also earned two postsecondary degrees in education at FAMU. She was married to the late Lee Walter Meeks, with whom she had one child, Lavonda Renee. Her special memories about Allen Subdivision were "the good relationships among the neighbors." She said, "Everyone was respectful. We all had the ability to work well with one another. We always helped each other in a time of need."

Mattie H. Mobley, 101, is the eldest of the 2014 honorees. She moved to Allen Subdivision in 1939. She and her husband, Arthur, lived on West Harrison Street, where they raised three children: Aramentha, Arthur Jr., and Gail. She was a master cosmetologist and owner of Mobley's Beauty Shop, a home-based business, and she moved in 1989 after selling her property, where a portion of the FAMU Pharmacy Building now stands. She says her fifty years spent in the neighborhood as a beautician were special because she had the honor of meeting many people throughout the years. She received many awards, certificates, and plaques as a community activist and participated in political, social, service, and civic organizations. She reported that she also "received the Doctor of Divinity from Smith Chapel College in Tallahassee." "Ms. Mattie" repeatedly expresses, "Allen Subdivision is the best neighborhood in Tallahassee, and all the children in Allen are mine! I loved that neighborhood. I never did see any police around. It was a nice neighborhood!"

Virginia Long Pinkney, 81, was born in Allen Subdivision. She is the granddaughter of Benjamin J. and Georgia "Sang" Long, a midwife who delivered many children in Allen. Virginia attended Lucy Moten Elementary School. She graduated from FAMU High School and received a bachelor of science degree from FAMU. She is married to H. B. Pinkney, PhD, with whom she has two children: Margaret and Zachary. She volunteered in the FAMU Athletic Ticket Office and held committee, board, and membership posts in church, civic, social, and service organizations. She shared special memories of time spent during her youth enjoying "all of the amenities of living near Florida A&M University."

Eva Clack Smith, 83, was born on Van Buren Street and later moved to Canal Street with her family. She married Otto B. Smith, and they raised three children: Keith, Dayna, and Randall. President of her class, Eva graduated from the Original Lincoln High School in 1949. Eva was a Lewis State Scholarship recipient of two hundred dollars per semester until graduating with a bachelor's degree in English from FAMU. There, as an honor student, she was named in *Who's Who in American Colleges and Universities*. She taught school at Griffin Junior High in Tallahassee for two years. For one year each, she also taught in Chipley, Florida, and in Connecticut. After military travel throughout Germany, she and her family moved to Fort Washington, Maryland, where she held numerous positions and retired in1993. Eva remembers knowing all the people in the immediate community and how they looked out for all children. She said, "We were raised in such a manner that we were responsible for what occurs in our community."

Charlie Conoly Smith, 81, lived in the 1500 block of South Bronough Street from birth. She married Jackson Smith, and they raised Ursula Smith Perry, Greg Stephen Smith, and Lowanda Smith. She attended Lucy E. Moten Elementary and FAMU High School. Smith attained a bachelor of science degree from FAMU. She held memberships in service organizations and served on several boards in Brevard County, where she worked for the Brevard County Public School Board before retiring. She remembers Smith's Jewelry Shop, the only Black jewelry store in Tallahassee; hearing music from FAMU Lee Hall and the band barracks; FAMU president J. R. E. Lee's riding his horse down the lane next to her house; the Fountainette; Campus Cleaners; the barracks at FAMU High with potbelly heaters in classrooms; red clay streets; and the way grown people were respected.

Doristine Williams Stephens, 81, is the wife of Clyde Stephens and mother of Clyde Jr., Michael, Keith, and Darrell (deceased). Born in Allen Subdivision, she attended Lucy E. Moten Elementary School, FAMU High School, and FAMU. Stephens worked for the Dade County School Board for thirty-one years. Her precious memories include growing up with and learning from her grandparents, going to church, and going to the Care Market in Smokey Hollow. She also remembers "attending activities at FAMU; watching basketball and football games; skating around the hills in the neighborhood; enjoying friends in Allen; modeling clothes for Mrs. Inez Hollis; and attending concerts at Lee Hall."

Francina Wanza, 83, began living in Allen Subdivision when she enrolled at Florida A&M College. During that time, she lived with Evelyn Lamb. She later married Charles Wanza, and together they raised five children. Four of her children—Deborah, Charles Jr., Howard, and Alicia—were born in Allen Subdivision, where her family lived for thirty-seven years. Her youngest child, Frank, was born in the Jake Gaither area. Wanza retired as an educator from the Leon County School System. She had worked several years at the FAMU and FSU bookstores. Wanza remembers "walking up muddy roads to go to school at FAMU."

Olivia Williams, 92, (deceased) resided in Allen Subdivision for many years, where she raised her two children, Patricia and Marva. She was a beautician and worked from her home on the corner of Jennings (Jakes and Patterson) and Melvin Streets. Williams provided much-needed housing for FAMU students at her home. She said that she had special memories of the FAMU students who boarded with her, and many of them visited and kept in touch with her for years after they graduated. She was an Eastern Star for over fifteen years and a member of the Democratic Women's Club. As an active member of Bethel AME Church for many years, she was a deaconess and an active member of many boards and organizations.

As a thriving, humble community of people who had faced enormous, longstanding challenges, the families of Allen Subdivision have achieved monumental feats. Among the 2014 Super Significant Seniors are citizens who reached unfathomable heights in their lives and careers in spite of their modest beginnings. Many earned college degrees and professional credentials. They also gave leadership and service to enrich the lives of others in their respective communities. As noted above, many of these Allenites received multiple achievement awards for their outstanding service.

12

In Spite of the Odds: Generations Excelled and Propelled

At least three generations of citizens have emerged from Allen residents since the inception of the community. With the lingering odds against them, and by normal social, economic, and psychological standards, most Allen kids would not have been expected to succeed in life. However, first-generation offspring of original Allen residents form an amazing array of prodigies who distinguished themselves with significant contributions to society. Granted, the outlook for social, economic, and career achievements of the latter generations has been far more optimistic than that for their parents, grandparents, adult relatives, and neighbors who lived in the community in the early 1900s. For their offspring, the range of educational opportunities, job prospects, employers, and employment sites have justly expanded exponentially, beyond the range afforded the early residents.

The scope of this review does not accommodate a listing of the achievements of every Allen descendant, nor does it include every accolade and award of the offspring cited. In addition to the accomplishments of the Super Significant Seniors, noted above, the list below cites achievements of a sampling of other individuals (between forty-six and seventy-six years of age) who were raised under the "Allen Effect." The information provided was self-reported by 2014 survey participants, individual interview respondents, achievers' relatives and other informants.

The extraordinary achievements of these Allen offspring at the peaks of their careers cover a wide range of fields in city, county, state, national, and international arenas. Some individuals may be listed in more than one category because of the nature of their achievements in multiple fields. Examples of the achievers, the streets on which they lived, and the areas in which they excelled include, but are not limited to the following.

Accounting

Nellie Paige Johnson (deceased) (Van Buren Street), State Department of Agriculture, Tallahassee, Florida, supervisor of accounting; leadership and service were also demonstrated in church organizations and auxiliaries, including the finance committee, mothers board, deaconess board, National Usher Congress, and in community and civic organizations, such as the Urban League, the Red Hatters, Order of Eastern Star, and others.

Lavern A. Washington (Melvin Street), assistant comptroller, assets management, FAMU; first African American student body president at Rickards High School in Tallahassee; led coalition of student body presidents in Leon County Public School System; director of Guideright, Tallahassee Alumni Chapter of Kappa Alpha Psi Fraternity Inc.; director of the Florida and Alabama Provincial Guideright Program; and adviser to the Alpha Zi Chapter/Tallahassee Alumni Chapter of Kappa Alpha Psi Fraternity, Inc.

Annarene Hicks Wineglass (Melvin Street), associate controller, FAMU, Tallahassee, Florida; earned a bachelor's degree in business administration and an MBA in management information at FAMU; member of the Tallahassee Alumni Chapter of Delta Sigma Theta Sorority.

Administrative and Executive Secretarial Services

Mary Alice Allison Allen (Hudson Street), administrative assistant in the School of Nursing at FAMU, from which she retired after thirty-five years of employment; completed certification in Office Administration and Services in the FAMU Comprehensive Education and Training Act (CETA) Program; secretary at Gethsemane Missionary Baptist Church for over fifty years; served on various church committees and was recipient of multiple awards for dedication and service at Gethsemane Church.

Phillippa Dorsey Floyd (Van Buren Street), executive secretary to the superintendent, Miami-Dade County Public Schools; retired in 2008 after over thirty years of service with the Miami-Dade School Board; secretary of the Miami Trinity Christian Methodist Episcopal Church for several years; recipient of multiple awards for dedicated service to the church.

Mary Frison Avant (South Bronough Street), secretary to court of appeals judge, second circuit, New York, New York.

Art

Earl Washington (South Bronough Street), supervisor of masonry for twenty-five years in the Grounds Department at FSU, where he received many merit awards as an exemplary employee; attained his bachelor's degree in fine arts and humanities at FAMU; received many "Best in Show" awards for his art productions; served as deacon at Gethsemane Missionary Baptist for thirty-seven years and chairman of the Deacon Board for multiple years.

Athletics/Sports

Adolph C. Hicks (Melvin Street), Coach of the Tallahassee Lady Thunders Semi-Pro Women's Basketball Team, Big Bend Coach of the Year (Twice), Coach/Teach of FAMU High School Girls and Boys Basketball Teams, Coach/Teacher at Leon and Rickards High Schools, Coach at Cobb Middle School. Carried FAMU High Girls' Basketball team to state competition twice.

James Long (Canal Street), football coach and teacher, North Shore High School, West Palm Beach, Florida; All-Conference/All-State high school running back; 1966 second-leading football scorer, FAMU.

Marcellus Long (South Boulevard Street), postman, FSU; maintenance supervisor, Housing Department (electric, plumbing, carpentry), FAMU; 1982 Father of the Year, Philadelphia Primitive Baptist Church; 2007 inductee, All National High School Basketball Hall of Fame; recipient, All Conference High School Basketball Award.

Weser Khufu (South Bronough Street), first to finish in Greensborough 4th of July Run, Tallahassee, Florida; featured in article and cover of *Gulf Wind Track Club Magazine*; finished sixth in the National 31 Mile Race, the second Floridian to finish.

Business Ownership

Melvin Beal (Melvin Street), CEO/owner, MBJ Communications (forty-two multimedia internet sites), Riverview, Florida.

Richard Jefferson (South Bronough Street), CEO/owner, VIP Star Spotlight Limousine Service.

Weser Khufu (South Bronough Street), CEO/owner, Pyramid Construction and Design.

Clarence Anderson (Van Buren Street), state-licensed building contractor, Anderson Construction; wrote degree programs at Central Florida Community College, Ocala, Florida.

Terrance Hinson (Melvin Street), CEO, Hinson Realty and Lion Share Management, Tallahassee, Florida.

Chemistry

Alexander Henry (Melvin Street), Ballistic Analyst III, Olin Corporation/St. Marks Division, General Dynamic in St. Marks, Florida.

Clergy and Religion

Chester L. Brown (Van Buren Street), minister, Concord AME Church; master's degree in theology, University of Georgia, 2002.

Clarence David Anderson, Sr. (deceased) (Van Buren Street), associate pastor, Family Life Christian Center, Tallahassee, Florida.

Annarene Wineglass (Melvin Street), ordained minister; Florida District of the AME Church.

Community/Neighborhood Leadership

Betty J. Pittman (Hudson Street), over ten years of community leadership, South Bronough Street Neighborhood Association; community coach, Pyramid Studios (Disability Health Care Services); National JTPA Certification as nursing assistant, Tallahassee, Florida.

Construction/General Contracting

Clarence Anderson (Van Buren Street), appointed to State Apprenticeship Council by Governor Reubin Askew.

Weser Khufu (Bronough Street), Florida certified general contractor; owner, Pyramid Construction and Design (thirty-five years); first African American to pass Leon County Contractor's Examination.

Education

Alton Farmer (Hudson Street), health, physical education, and driver's education teacher, Leon County District Schools; Dedicated Teacher Award Recipient, Leon County Teachers Association.

Irene Gilliam (Melvin Street), English professor, Tallahassee Community College; published author, *Never Too Late for Love*.

Louise Gilliam Hannah (deceased) (Melvin Street), English teacher, Fairview Middle School; Eponym Annual Award for Student Exemplifying Outstanding Achievement, Fairview Middle School.

Adolph Hicks (Melvin Street), teacher and coach, Leon County School Board; All Big Bend Coach of the Year (two years); member, Alpha Zi Chapter, Kappa Alpha Psi Fraternity Inc.

Cherry Lawrence (Canal Street), teacher (thirty-eight years), Leon County School District; Teacher of the Year (twice), Pineview Elementary School; master's degree in elementary education.

Educational Leadership and Supervision

Larry Allison (Hudson Street), assistant principal, Pinellas County School Board, St. Petersburg, Florida; master's degree in educational administration, Nova University.

Deloris Massey Harpool (Hudson Street), policy director, State Board of Community Colleges; director, Florida College Reach Out Program; recipient, Lifetime Achievement Award, Florida Association of Community Colleges Equity Commission; honoree, *Who's Who Among Students in American Colleges and Universities*; honoree, Women in Leadership in the State of Florida; honoree, Unsung Heroes in the Black Community, Publix Supermarkets, Tallahassee, Florida; Member, Delta Kappa Omega Chapter of Alpha Kappa Alpha (AKA) Sorority Inc.; Life and Golden member of AKA; member, Kappa Delta Pi Honorary Society; honoree, Outstanding Young Women of America; Certified Public Manager (CPM), Rutgers University, Rutgers, New Jersey.

Jennie Smith Collette (South Bronough Street), principal, Evergreen School District; specialist in multicultural education, Alumrock School District, San Jose, California; member, Human Relations Commission; president, board of directors, Martin Luther King Jr. School; member, Task Force to Combat Crime and Drugs; president/charter member, National Council of Negro Women, San Jose, California; honoree, Wall of Distinction, Department of Education, FAMU; White House honoree, National Blue Ribbon Schools, Washington, DC.

Lanell Mills McCaskill (Hudson Street), assistant principal, Pineview Elementary School; 2014 Volunteer of the Year, Pineview Elementary School, Tallahassee, Florida; Phi Delta Kappa, Honorary Society, FAMU; Silver Star Member and Committee Leader, Delta Kappa Omega Chapter, Alpha Kappa Alpha Sorority Inc.

Napoleon Mills (Hudson Street), PhD in education; area center director, Vocational Technical Center, Manatee County School District; adjunct professor, Argosy University, Sarasota, Florida and Western Governors University, Brandon, Utah; ordained deacon, St. Mary Missionary Baptist Church, Bradenton, Florida; chairman of the board of commissioners, Bradenton Housing Authority, Bradenton, Florida.

Family and Consumer Sciences

Mildred Gilliam Alexander (Melvin Street), director, special research, Family and Consumer Sciences, FSU; teacher, Leon County District School Board.

Fire Science and Service

Richard Jefferson (South Bronough Street), firefighter and engineer, Tallahassee Fire Department; Heroic Award for Life Saving and Bravery Award, Tallahassee Fire Department.

Michael Randolph (deceased) (Van Buren Street), fire chief, Gainesville, Florida; US Fire Administrator, National Fire Academy; instructor, Fire Science Department, Tallahassee Community College; assistant chief of training, Tallahassee Fire Department; nominee, Top Fire Educator of the Year and National Fire Chief of the Year; commendations as committee chairman for numerous committees, Tallahassee Alumni Chapter of Kappa Alpha Psi Fraternity Inc.

Food Service Management and Support

Earlene Allison Farmer (Hudson Street), dietary aide, Tallahassee Memorial Hospital (TMH); teacher aide, Bond and Pineview Elementary Schools; recipient, TMH Dedicated Service Award in Dietary Services; served as a designated mother of the St. Paul Primitive Baptist Church in Crawfordville, Florida, for many years; award recipient for excellent and dedicated service at the 2015 Allen Subdivision Reunion.

Mary Brewster Hargis (Hudson Street), food services manager, Pineview and John G. Riley Elementary Schools; Also served at SAIL and Second Chance Alternative Schools; Established the first food service program at the Second Chance School; recipient, 2009–2010 Recognition Award for dedication and service to the students, mission, and vision of the James H. Rickards High School; member, Red Hatters of Tallahassee, Florida; alumnus of FAMU; member, FAMU 220 Athletic Club.

International, National, and Regional Consulting

Deloris Mills Massey Harpool (Hudson Street), consultant, US Agency for International Development (USAID), Johannesburg, South Africa; Southern Regional Education Board (SREB), Doctoral Fellows Program, Atlanta, Georgia; published author and editor, US Institute for Services to Education, Washington, DC.

Alexander Henry (Melvin Street), consultant, engineering and technical advisor on proper chemical mix of gunpowder, Federal Republic of Yugoslavia.

Journalism and Mass Communications

Melvin Beal (Melvin Street), general manager, WVUP TV; broadcaster and freelance reporter, Entertainment and Sports Programming Network (ESPN) TV, Tampa, Florida; chairman, media and public relations, NAACP, Tampa Chapter, Tampa, Florida; reporter, FAMU nationally aired (70+) stories, ESPN and Black Entertainment Television (BET); and TV news reporter, Columbia Broadcasting Service (CBS) Tampa Affiliate.

Nancy Jefferson Godette (South Bronough Street), social editor, *Capital Outlook* newspaper, Tallahassee, Florida; teacher, vocational education, State of Georgia; recipient, Emory O. Jackson Award for Outstanding Performance in Journalism; member, Delta Kappa Omega Chapter, Alpha Kappa Alpha Sorority Inc.

Law

Remus Allen (deceased) (Hudson Street), jurist doctorate, practicing attorney, Tallahassee, Florida.

Law Enforcement and Corrections

Chester L. Brown (West Van Buren Street), corrections officer sergeant, Florida Division of Corrections.

Raymond Henry (Melvin Street), sergeant, Tallahassee Police Department; recipient, Award for Bravery/Life Saving (three years), Tallahassee Police Department; 1995 Black

Achievement Award in Law Enforcement, NAACP, Tallahassee, Florida; organizer, Tallahassee Black Police Officers United for Justice.

Local, State, Regional, and National Church Leadership

Jerrlyne Allen Jackson, PhD. (Hudson Street), graduate, FAMU and FSU; teacher for forty years, business education, FAMU; "Teacher of the Year" twice; retired in 2003 as professor emeritus; served in multiple leadership positions at Greater Mt. Zion Church; in the state and national Primitive Baptist Church Convention, actively served for over fifty-five years in over nine leadership positions, collectively, including editor of the national convention's magazine, director of the publishing board for the National Primitive Baptist Convention, president of the State Primitive Baptist Women's Congress, president of the Ladies Art and Social Club Inc. for six years, president of the Jake Gaither Neighborhood Association, first Black president of the Florida Business Education Association in 1988, and member of Alpha Kappa Alpha Sorority Inc., Delta Kappa Omega Chapter.

Mable Allison Webster (Hudson Street), held varying leadership positions during many years of service to the church, including missionary secretary, member of the usher board and deaconess of Mt. Pleasant Missionary Baptist Church in Tallahassee, and president of the deaconess board at Gethsemane Missionary Baptist Church in Tallahassee; for several years, held the positions of Mother and president of the deaconess board at Elizabeth Baptist Church in Monticello, Florida; before retirement, employed in Tallahassee as supervisor of cosmetics with Walgreens Pharmacy.

Medicine

Ernest Hoffman, MD (Palmer Avenue), physician, Student Health Services, FAMU, Tallahassee, Florida; medical director, Leon County Health Department, Tallahassee, Florida; honoree, *Who's Who Among Students in Colleges and Universities*; member, Alpha Kappa Mu Honor Society; National Merit Scholar.

Military Service

Remus Allen (deceased) (Hudson Street), commissioned ROTC officer, FAMU; honoree, Distinguished Military Service, US Army.

Allen Beal (deceased) (Melvin Street), retired military officer, first African American Grand Marshal, 2010 Tallahassee Veterans Day Parade; varying commendations in the US Army.

Ronald Beasley (Melvin Street), captain, US Navy; first African American Captain, Navy ROTC program, FAMU, Tallahassee. Florida.

James Gosby (Melvin Street), logistics program manager, US Air Force; employed thirty-six years by the federal government, with eight years as staff sergeant, US Air Force.

Georgia Conoly Labadie (Bronough Street), colonel, US Army Reserve.

Nursing and Health Education

Joy Anderson, PhD (Melvin Street), doctorate in health education, Texas A&M University; executive director, Gadsden County Healthy Start Coalition; 2012 Woman of the Year, Gadsden Chapter, National Hook-Up of Black Women Inc.

Georgia Conoly Labadie, EdD (Bronough Street), doctorate in nursing education; dean, School of Nursing, FAMU; honoree, Nursing Hall of Fame, Teachers College, Columbia University; fellow, Academy of Nursing Education, National League for Nursing; Outstanding Alumna in Nursing, FAMU National Alumni Association; honoree, Gallery of Distinction, School of Nursing, FAMU.

Delores Brooks Lawson, PhD (South Boulevard Street), doctorate in nursing, University of Alabama at Birmingham; master's in nursing, University of Florida; bachelor of science in nursing, FAMU; associate dean, undergraduate program, School of Nursing, FAMU; inductee, Gallery of Distinction and 2000 Outstanding Alumnus, School of Nursing, FAMU; member, Delta Sigma Theta Sorority Inc.

Psychology

Juanita Pittman Bivins, EdS (South Bronough Street), doctorate in school psychology; school psychologist, Duval County Public Schools (thirty-two years); recipient, Accommodation Medal—Cuban Embargo Crisis, US Army; honoree, *Who's Who Among Business Professionals*; honoree, Community Service Award—Connecting Young Females with Futures, Duval County Teen Parent Program; honoree, High Achiever in Crisis Intervention Services, Jacksonville, Florida.

Public Service

Franklin Graham (deceased) (West Van Buren Street), president of the Student Government Association, FAMU; first student member and first African American to serve on the Florida Board of Regents, governing board of the ten state universities.

Collectively, the individuals cited in this document and others who lived in Allen Subdivision portray an incredible success story. Not all of them experienced the same level of struggles or success. However, most shared common social and economic difficulties as African Americans who survived against tough odds in Tallahassee, Florida. Common threads of sage advice, communal love and protection, and unrelenting encouragement from the community elders, as well as personal ambition and drive, proved beneficial to all reared within the boundaries of the neighborhood.

The Allen Effect did not end with those reared in the community. Children were expected to do better than their parents and grandparents. They were advised to grow up "to be somebody." Over at least three generations, the lessons of the Allen Village Builders continue to resonate. A steady stream of achievers has come from these generations.

The progenies of Allen-raised residents have soared to unfathomable heights. Collectively, they have claimed their places among accomplished medical doctors, inventors, engineers, bureau chiefs, assistant fire chiefs, corporate executives, licensed practical nurses, medical technologists, radiologists, electronic technicians, politicians, authors and journalists, marketing professionals, attorneys, primary and secondary school principals, administrators, teachers, university professors and presidents, computer systems experts, and leaders in international sororities and fraternities and in other distinguished organizations.

Allen: An Incubator and Pathway to Success

As a community, Allen Subdivision has proved itself to be a noteworthy neighborhood where significant business, homeownership, education, and leadership were available, encouraged, supported, and developed. Its products represented a communal vision for citizens who emerged as achievers from a modest neighborhood in Tallahassee, Florida. Allen has appropriately utilized valuable resources. As a unified community of faith and hope, it has sustained life and livelihood for all community partners concerned.

Among the early residents, important foundations were laid for scores of citizens to push through social, civic, racial, economic, and environmental obstacles, ultimately making significant contributions to society. A clear message emerges: With faith in God; strong moral character; support of a nurturing, bonded community; love of neighbors; respect for one's parents, elders, self, and others; a willing spirit; and hard work and perseverance, one can overcome the odds.

William Proctor, Jr., 2022 Chair of the Leon County Board of Commissioners, shared his opinion about this cherished community. He states "Allen subdivision captures the epitome of an American community that exhibited the pride, sacrifices, and commitment of families focusing on upward mobility. The success of their focus and struggles are evidenced and enshrined in the outcomes of the lives of many children and grandchildren. To God be the glory for the positive layer of history."

APPENDIX

*Key Influences, Players and Outcomes
in the Development and Communication
of the Allen Subdivision Story*

The study of the history of the community called Allen Subdivision, or Allen, in Tallahassee, Florida, was initiated among current and previous Allen residents in 2014. This was subsequent to the launching of the Capital Cascade Trail and FAMU Way Project. The project is sponsored by the Blueprint Intergovernmental Agency (BIA) comprised of city and county officials in Tallahassee. Allen residents also refer to the project as the FAMU Way Redevelopment Project.

Call to Action

The Allen community sprang into action when Cherry Lawrence, owner of a Canal Street property being affected by the redevelopment project, read about the project in the Tallahassee Democrat. She called Carrie Poole, communications coordinator for the City of Tallahassee, and informed Poole that she did not believe other Allen residents had received information about the groundbreaking for the project. Lawrence further asked to be placed on the city's mailing list for additional updates.

In the meantime, Lawrence contacted Lavern Washington, a previous resident of Melvin Street in Allen Subdivision. Washington had previously been a member of a group that had planned a 2013 reunion of Allen residents. Along with Washington and Lawrence, the reunion planning group included Deborah Washington, Lori Henry,

Melvin Beal (via telephone conferencing), Weser Khufu, Earlene Allison Farmer, and Walter Godette.

By consensus, the group acknowledged that the composition of the Allen neighborhood was slowly changing from families to students. The group noted physical encroachment by FAMU and by the city and county in the area. Recognizing the reality of change that comes with urban progress, the concerned stakeholders established that immediate involvement in the FAMU Way project was critical. They decided to ensure that other Allen previous and current residents were informed and would get involved to secure a forum for their voice in the direction and impact of the local project.

Lavern Washington accepted responsibility to lead the group with a temporary change of focus from the planning of another reunion. The new agenda was to ensure the preservation of history and attainment of commemorative markers for Allen as part of the local FAMU Way Redevelopment Project, with Allen's direct input. The ultimate mission was to be sure the project would in part highlight the existence of Allen Subdivision as a historic, once-thriving, significantly self-contained African American community.

The group of concerned citizens gained momentum and grew to approximately twenty active participants. They adopted as their temporary title the Adhoc Committee for Preservation of the History of the Community Called Allen Subdivision. The title was later shortened to the Allen Subdivision History Committee.

Leader Washington invited Carrie Poole to the group's meetings to inform Allenites of the progress of the FAMU Way venture. The group advised Poole that it was important to have the city hear from Allen community stakeholders. It was further essential that the history be written and told from the perspective of the residents of the internal community. In addition to providing multiple updates, Poole expressed the need for a narrative describing the Allen Subdivision history.

Washington requested Deloris Massey Harpool, a previous resident of Allen, to take the lead in producing the written history for the community. Initially, minimal information was available. Still, Harpool and the committee maintained commitment to produce their own story internally, including documentation from official external sources, where available and possible.

Harpool agreed to conduct extensive research and write the Allen story, provided the concerned Allen group was willing to help by documenting their experiences. A preliminary outline of proposed topics was presented, and the group agreed that the topics were desirable and appropriate. The factors identified would drive the questions to be asked of informants in group discussions, on a written survey instrument, in individual interviews and in audio and TV recordings.

Multiple efforts were launched to ensure a comprehensive, robust, and substantive internal review of the neighborhood's history. Inquiries began with a city map search to identify the geographic site of reference. Simultaneously, the Allen History Committee organized an event at which oral histories from local surviving senior citizens who had lived or reared children in Allen would be recorded.

The Elders Have Spoken

On October 19, 2014, the committee invited a group of elders to give personal testimonies while also being honored as esteemed members of the Allen family. The committee treated the elder guests to a museum tour, followed by a "Sunday Afternoon Chat" and a special reception in their honor. The event was held at the FAMU James Eaton/Carrie Meek Southeastern Regional Black Archives Research Center and Museum. The average age for this group of informants was eighty-six. In this group were fourteen participants: four males and ten females.

Super Significant Senior history informants at "Sunday Afternoon Chat." (2014). Image courtesy of Earl Washington.

While interacting with the elder informants, the History Committee assigned to them the title Super Significant Seniors, or the SSS Group. This title was based upon the elders' enthusiastic participation, their substantive comments, and their incredible account of their days in Allen. It was also fitting for their value to the Allen family. The elders' comments were audio and video recorded, and later captured in a written transcript. Their input, along with other information and data gathered from diverse sources, provided a substantial beginning for the account of Allen's history.

Documentation of the Allen Experience

To secure documentation from additional residents who had lived in the community from its inception, a thirty-eight-item survey was drafted and proposed. The instrument was adopted in early October 2014 and administered in a November survey session to a second group of informants. In a letter dated October 9, 2014, Lavern Washington invited current and previous residents to participate in the planned session. To inform them and encourage their involvement in the creation of written history about Allen, Washington wrote,

> As you may be aware, the City of Tallahassee is moving swiftly toward the re-development of Van Buren Street and FAMU Way (the old Canal Street). With the intent to extend FAMU Way to Lake Bradford Road, a part of the City's plan will affect the geographic area we call "Allen Subdivision." Some houses in the area already have been demolished, due to the Duval/ Bronough Street extension, where the Thomas Bridge was erected. As we anticipate further growth projects by Florida A&M University (FAMU) and by the City, we find it critical that we act now as a collective body to ensure that the rich history of Allen is not lost or forgotten.

The surveys were administered on November 9, 2014, at the FAMU Developmental Research School in Tallahassee. A diverse group of residents attended the session and provided written responses regarding their Allen experiences. Of the eighty individuals invited, forty-three (54 percent) attended the session and completed the survey. Of this group, fifteen (35 percent) were males and twenty-eight (65 percent) were females. One of the survey participants was eighty-two, and another was eighty-three years of age.

Eight additional survey respondents who had not participated in the initial survey session completed the survey in a separate session held at the home of Betty Pittman. Minus the two seniors, the ages of participants ranged from forty-six to seventy-six. In total, the average age of all survey informants was sixty-four.

Six volunteers from Allen helped to tally the survey responses. In groups of twos, the Tally Team counted and double checked one another's counts to ensure accurate recording of the collective informants' responses. Lavern Washington provided energizing refreshments. The Tally Team included Queen Bruton, Earlene Allison Farmer, Nancy Jefferson Godette, Mary Brewster Hargis, Deloris Mills Harpool, and Cherry Lawrence. Harpool developed a narrative summary from the data recorded. Queen Bruton and Cherry Lawrence reviewed and provided initial edits for the summary.

Subsequent to the survey information collected from the group of middle-aged residents, another document was developed based upon oral histories provided by six seniors who agreed to be recorded on television. The televised session took place at 11:30 a.m. on Tuesday, May 12, 2015, in the School of Journalism and Graphic Communications Building on the campus of Florida A&M University.

The FAMU TV20 guests included six of the elders (eighty years and older), most of whom had previously participated in the October 2014 "Sunday Afternoon Chat." Two of the participants were males, James Cullen "J. C." Lawrence and Dennis Jefferson; and four were females, Susie Brown, Queen Bruton, Mattie Mobley, and Virginia Pinkney. Dr. O. Sylvia Lamar Sheffield was the FAMU TV20 host who interviewed the seniors in the televised session.

The 2015 Reunion: Igniting Memories/Affirming a Legacy

The Adhoc Committee decided that a 2015 neighborhood reunion was in order. The group agreed that it would be timely and important to honor members of the SSS Group at the event. They designed the reunion with several goals in mind: to allow all participants to have fun and share memories; to increase knowledge of Allen's history; to pay tribute to deceased Allen residents and to allow surviving Allen seniors to receive recognition with their contemporaries while sharing their personal stories. The information gathered allowed for additional input for the community's collective history.

Serving nearly one hundred participants, the three day reunion was held from July 16, to July 18, 2015. It began with a Friday afternoon reception and ended with Sunday worship at the newly constructed Gethsemane Missionary Baptist Church in Tallahassee's South City. At the Friday reception, participants registered and began socializing on the open lot where the Pittman Boarding House once stood.

Saturday activities included a morning photo shoot to capture pictures of the 2015 reunion participants in their specially designed T-shirts.

Allen Subdivision Reunion participants at Lake Anita Favors Plaza on FAMU Way, previous Canal Street (2015). Courtesy of Earl Washington.

The Saturday afternoon banquet at the Smith-Williams Center included a Jeopardy game to test participants' memories and provide newly uncovered history facts. In the same session, a preliminary document from members of the committee was distributed describing each of the Super Significant Senior honorees. (For purposes of this publication, information was subsequently gathered directly from the honorees, validated, and recorded from mid-September to the end of October 2015 via follow-up telephone interviews conducted by Queen Bruton, Cherry Lawrence, and Deloris Harpool.)

A segment of the program was designated as a memorial ceremony for Village Builders who had passed away. To honor the deceased, Earl Washington presented an inaugural Memorial Registry for display. The beautifully designed wood-stained commemorative board featured small metal plates identifying all known deceased Village Builders and previous residents. The board was later delivered for storage in the Carrie P. Meeks unit of the FAMU Archives and Museum.

A highlight of the Saturday event was when the planning group treated the eldest surviving Allenites to a special moment on the dance floor. The theme for this segment was the "Beauty and the Beast Moment". Participating senior "beauties" were coupled with less seasoned neighborhood "beasts" they collectively helped to raise. At the beginning, the couples danced to the slow, melodious 1991 song - Beauty and the Beast - by Peabo Bryson and Celine Dion. Suddenly, the music shifted to a much faster 1965 selection by R & B singer, James Brown – "I Feel Good!" The seniors were tickled as they immediately rose to the occasion to 'cut the rug' and flaunt their moves!

Reunion "Beauty and Beast" Moment: Mrs. Inez Hicks (left) dances with her son, Alvin Hicks (right). Image courtesy of Earl Washington.

Reunion "Beauty and Beast" Moment: Samuel Long, Jr. (left) dances with his aunt, Mrs. Virginia Long Pinkney (right). Image courtesy of Earl Washington.

Reunion "Beauty and Beast" Moment: Lois Gilbert (left) dances with a neighborhood senior mentor, Mr. Leroy Baker (right). Image courtesy of Earl Washington.

Reunion "Beauty and Beast" Moment: Mrs. Susie Brown (left) dances with son, Hubert Brown, Jr. (right). Image courtesy of Earl Washington.

Georgia Conoly Labadie (left) and Queen Hargrett Bruton (right) relish memories of the good ole days at reunion cook-out held at historic site of Pittman Boarding House on S. Bronough Street.(2015) Courtesy of Earl Washington.

Other data-collection methods involved face-to-face interviews and additional telephone interviews. From early March to mid-June of 2015, personal interviews were conducted with seven consenting individuals. Six of these individuals (four females and two males) had been reared in the Allen community.

One telephone interview was conducted and recorded by Deloris Harpool with Dorothy Carroll, a Caucasian female who was a previous owner of property in Carroll's and Carroll's South Subdivisions. Mrs. Carroll was the wife of Fred Carroll Jr., who was widely known for interacting with and collecting rent from the tenants for his father, Fred Carroll Sr., the initial developer of two of the larger official subdivisions in Allen. Additional interviews were conducted with Allen Subdivision achievers in early February of 2016.

It should be pointed out that the information presented in this internal review does not include every individual who lived or owned property in Allen Subdivision. Nor does it reflect the personal experience of every single informant. Rather, in addition to information from published, legal sources, it reflects patterns of information provided by and corroborated through many Allen residents. It includes the preponderance of responses most commonly submitted by survey respondents, oral history testimonies, individual interview informants, and memoirs of the author, collectively.

Overall, the study involved comments, photos, and input from ninety informants (unduplicated headcount). Eighty-seven of these individuals were current or previous Allen residents. One was the owner of two of the legal subdivisions in the community, and two other informants were observers of a segment of the Allen story through their involvement in one of the churches in the neighborhood.

Based upon input from all individual informants—along with the review of relevant literature and examination of legal documents, including Tallahassee City Commission Resolutions, building permits, newspaper articles, maps and property deeds—a documented, detailed story of Allen was created and is included herein.

Civic Engagement and Collaboration

The City of Tallahassee and Leon County responded to the Allen Subdivision stakeholders' efforts and concerns in several ways. While the internal Allen study was underway, the city and county Blueprint Intergovernmental Agency (BIA) hired a team of FAMU history professors to study the neighborhoods and commercial districts along the entirety of the FAMU Way Corridor. Allen residents participated in the interviews conducted by the FAMU team. In addition, parts of the internal Allen story were shared with the FAMU professors as a means to support their project and ensure the inclusion of key historical facts about Allen Subdivision.

There was a difference in the focus of the two simultaneous studies. The FAMU team's study provided an overarching review of multiple communities connected by FAMU Way. The internal Allen Subdivision study was designed specifically to provide a detailed, deep-dive review of the Allen story. From both studies, the city heard the voices of Allen.

Sharing and promotion of the Allen neighborhood story did not stop there. The internal Allen effort continued and expanded. Based upon the volume of information collected, the amount of research conducted and encouragement from a local citizen, it was determined that Allen's story deserved to be published. With available and extensive documented details, a comprehensive manuscript was developed for purposes of publication and broad dissemination.

In the meantime, the BIA invited residents from the Allen community to give ongoing input in its redevelopment project via the BIA Working Group. The agency invited Lavern Washington, Queen Bruton, and Deloris Harpool to serve in this advisory capacity. Earl Washington, another previous Allen resident, was later invited to serve. The role of the Working Group was to help select the specific information and types of interpretive displays to appropriately commemorate the history of the residential and commercial districts along the FAMU Way Corridor. Coordinated by Tatiana Daguillard, BIA planner, the group would serve until all interpretive displays and content were in place.

As a member of the Working Group, the Allen researcher shared a copy of the detailed Allen manuscript to help inform the topics and content for consideration by the BIA Working Group in completing its project. Along with information from other sources, the working group adopted significant information from the internal Allen study. Consultant Altamese Barnes, along with Harpool and other contributors collected images that enhanced the Allen narrative. The BIA conducted at least two community engagement meetings to solicit citizens' input and to ensure validation of the information and types of displays being planned.

Tangible Outcomes

By 2018 the Blueprint Intergovernmental Agency had designated a two-sided information box at the corner of West Van Buren and South Adams Streets. The east side of the box featured a welcome message and an overview of the history of Allen Subdivision. The information posted was taken directly from the internal Allen Subdivision study. In addition, way-finders were raised on poles along FAMU Way providing directions to the Allen community. These installations represented the first historical markers publically posted in Tallahassee about Allen Subdivision. With these public displays, the Allen group had executed its commitment to provide a resident-driven narrative about Allen.

The BIA's implementation plan currently reflects future Allen Subdivision interpretive markers along FAMU Way between Adams Street and Martin Luther King Jr. Boulevard. Some of the markers would present narratives about life in and the legacy of the neighborhood. Among other displays, the BIA's plan includes art installations and a marker specifically designated to celebrate the previous African American owned businesses in Allen. The composite BIA History and Culture Trail would include some of the same types of information and displays in other historical neighborhoods and commercial districts along the full corridor. The project is scheduled to be completed by the end of Spring 2023.

The internal Allen group initiated other efforts related to the essence of the community. On June 25, 2022, a historic site was unveiled and dedicated at the corner of S. Bronough Street and Jakes and Patterson Street to help communicate details about a notable Allen Family. Current and previous Allen residents secured funding for the site, which features a commemorative bench and a state marker honoring Willie and Carrie T. Pittman, parents of the Late Congresswoman, Carrie Pittman Meek. This historic display was funded by a Neighborhood Partnership Program grant, Financed by the Tallahassee Community Redevelopment Agency (CRA) and Administered by the City of Tallahassee's Neighborhood Affairs Division.

Walter Godette served as the newly elected chairman of the Allen History Committee that planned, coordinated and executed the unveiling ceremony for the Pittman markers. Other committee members included Joy Anderson, Diane Bellamy, Susie Brown, Melvina Davis, Nancy Godette, Mary Hargis, Deloris Harpool, Adolph Hicks, Cherry Lawrence, Marcellus Long, Marsetta McCants, Edna McGhee (deceased), Virginia Pinkney, Eva Parker, Betty Pittman, Cephus Staten, Earl Washington, Lavern Washington, Mable Webster, Willie Webster, Anita Wilson and Annarene Wineglass.

The Allen Subdivision History Committee sponsored multiple events to acquire extensive research and documentation about Allen. The Allen group was committed to get into a position to communicate to local leaders and others credible information about the essence of life in Allen, the noteworthy successes of previous Allen residents and the existence of Black owned Allen businesses. Without the internal committee's work and sacrifices, there would not be rich narratives coming from the internal Allen group that would help to enable historic markers being planned for FAMU Way by the Blueprint Intergovernmental Agency. Nor, would there be unveiling ceremonies in the neighborhood during this current period in Allen's history.

Since 2015, Lavern Washington, as leader of the History Committee, had played a key role in the initial steps toward honoring Carrie Pittman Meek. By September 2015, under Washington's leadership, the History Committee had voted that Meek was the most accomplished person who had grown up or lived in Allen and the individual who should be the most highlighted in Allen history. From April 2015 through September 2015, Washington met with Andrew Chin, Dean of the FAMU School of Architecture to seek ideas on tangible markers that might be pursued to honor Meek. Washington further communicated with the appropriate city staff to secure the electronic application and petition required to rename a street in the Allen community. In May 2015, as leader of the History Committee, Washington also had requested County Commissioner Bill Proctor's help in the project. In September 2015, he further communicated with the Pittman family to attain support.

With the required local endorsements that Betty Pittman had secured from Allen neighborhood residents and owners, Lavern Washington and Betty Pittman delivered the completed application to the appropriate city staff for processing in 2015. Unfortunately, the initial application did not get key endorsements and was pulled from the City Commission's agenda. However, shortly after the 2022 unveiling of the bench and marker at the site of the Pittman Boarding House, the revised application bearing the revised requested street name of Carrie Pittman Meek was submitted.

In addition, as representatives of the internal Allen History Committee, Betty Pittman and this author appeared before the Tallahassee City Commission and the Leon County Board of Commissioners, collectively, to request support for the renaming of a portion of S. Bronough Street. At the Allen History Committee's meeting of June 25, 2022, under the newly appointed chairman, Walter Godette, the Allen street naming sub-committee reported progress as a result of yet another historic action to which the History Committee had contributed.

As of September 13, 2022, the Tallahassee City Commission and the Board of Leon County Commissioners had approved the renaming of a segment of S. Bronough Street to the "Carrie Pittman Meek Street." The renaming ceremony was scheduled to be held November 4, 2022.

Among local officials who have expressed appreciation for the community-based efforts that led to tangible Allen Subdivision outcomes, one leader writes,

> As Mayor Pro Tem of the City, I am honored to recognize the author for producing this epic literary work capturing the history and culture of Allen Subdivision, a once thriving Black community. We have witnessed the demise of neighborhoods like this across our community. So, we encourage vigilance among local citizens like the Allen group to capture their history for present and future generations, and to continue bringing their concerns on a timely basis to the attention of city, county and state policy makers.
>
> **—Curtis Richardson, Mayor Pro Tem, City of Tallahassee**
> Chairman, Blueprint Intergovernmental Agency Board of Directors

REFERENCES

Allen Subdivision Reunion Committee. "Allen Subdivision's Outstanding Athletes of Yesteryears." *Reunion Booklet.* June 9, 2007, p. 13.

Area Views of Parcels in the Geographic Area Called Allen Subdivision. Tallahassee Leon County GIS/Department of Development Support and Environmental Management, Development Services Division, Tallahassee, Florida.

"Baker's Pharmacy Through the Ages." WCTV. January 17, 2005. http://www.wctv.tv/home/headlines/1358276.html (site discontinued)

Bivins, Juanita Pittman (granddaughter of Willie and Carry Tanzy Pittman), in discussion with the author, January 10, 2018.

Brown, Susie (long-term neighbor of Willie and Carry Tanzy Pittman and witness to 1956 cross burning on Jennings Street in Allen Subdivision), in discussions with the author, January 22 and 29, 2018.

Bruton, Q. H. (Super Significant Senior of Allen Subdivision and Allen Subdivision Achiever), in discussions with the author, September 17, 2015–October 27, 2015, and February 7–8, 2016.

Building Permits (1940–1955). City of Tallahassee Growth Management Department, Office of Records Management, Tallahassee, Florida.

"Capital Drive-In." Cinema Treasures. Accessed December 3, 2014 http://cinematreasures.org/theaters/33475.

Carroll, Dorothy R. (previous owner of Carroll and Carroll South tracts of land) in discussion with the author, October 21, 2014.

"Education and Training: History and Timelines." US Department of Veterans Affairs. (n.d.) https://www.benefits.va.gov/gibill/history.asp (site discontinued)

Estimate of Allen Subdivision Acreage (June 10, 2015), Tallahassee Leon County GIS/Department of Development Support and Environmental Management, Development Services Division.

"FAMU Way: Project Overview." City of Tallahassee. Accessed December 30, 2020. https://www.talgov.com/projects/famuway-proj-overview.aspx

Filmed Interview of Selected Super Significant Seniors of Allen Subdivision, (May 12, 2015), Florida A&M University, School of Journalism and Graphic Communication, TV20 Studio.

"Fire-Destroyed Building to Reopen." *The Famuan*. November 17, 1994. Vol. 80, no. 10, p. 9.

Florida A&M University. "History of Florida A&M University." Accessed August 14, 2015. https://www.famu.edu/about-famu/history/index-old.php

Florida Department of Transportation, 1985. Maxwell Samuel Thomas Bridge, Contract Number 55350-3501, Tallahassee, Florida.

"Florida in the Depression." Florida History Internet Center. (n.d.) http://floridahistory.org/depression.htm

"Florida Polk's Tallahassee City Directory." 1948–1966. R. L. Polk & Company Publishers.

Funeral Services of Carrie Tansy Pittman. December 2, 1966. Philadelphia Primitive Baptist Church, Tallahassee, Florida.

Harpool, D. M. "Sunday Afternoon Chat," (Transcribed by My'Eisha Penn), Tallahassee, Florida, October 19, 2014.

"History of Gethsemane Missionary Baptist Church." Gethsemane Missionary Baptist Church, Tallahassee, Florida. Accessed March 16, 2018

"History." St. Michael and All Angels Episcopal Church, Tallahassee, Florida. (n.d.)

"The Honorable Carrie P. Meek." The History Makers. June 19, 2001. http://www.thehistorymakers.org/biography/honorable-carrie-p-meek

"The Importance of Having Strong Communities." Borough of Dunmore Pennsylvania, Lackawanna County. April 25, 2017. https://dunmorepa.gov/news/importance-strong-communities

Lawrence, C. D. Notes on Telephone Interviews with Selected Super Significant Seniors of Allen Subdivision. September 17, 2015–October 27, 2015.

Lorusso, Lesa. "American Vernacular Architecture: The Shotgun Style in Florida." The Florida Historical Society. June 13, 2012. https://myfloridahistory.org/preservation/american-vernacular-architecture-shotgun-style-florida.

Map of Carroll's South Subdivision (1943), Leon County Court, Tallahassee Leon County Florida, Plat Book 2, p. 115

Map of Carroll's Subdivision (1936), Leon County Court, Tallahassee Leon County Florida, Plat Book 2, p. 68

Map of College View Subdivision (1926), Leon County Court, Tallahassee Leon County Florida, Plat Book 2, p. 21

Map of Morrill Heights Subdivision (1914), Leon County Court, Tallahassee Leon County Florida, Plat Book 1, p. 2

Map of Palmer's Addition South Subdivision (1908) Leon County Court, Tallahassee Leon County Florida, Plat Book N.N., p. 598

Map of Taylor Development (1946), Leon County Court, Tallahassee Leon County Florida, Official Record 862, P. 228 and Official Record Book 76, p. 325

Map Title, Leon County Property Appraiser's Office, Tallahassee, Florida. November 6, 2017.

Margo, Robert A. "Teacher Salaries in Black and White: Pay Discrimination in the Southern Classroom." National Bureau of Economic Research, University of Chicago Press. January 1990. p. 54. www.nber.org/chapters/c8794

McAlester, V. S. *A Field Guide to American Houses*. New York: Alfred A. Knopf, a Division of Random House, 2017. pp. 551, 567, 587, and 597.

McAlester, V. S. *A Field Guide to American Houses*: *The Definitive Guide to Identifying and Understanding America's Domestic Architecture*. New York: Alfred A. Knopf, a Division of Random House, 2014. pp. 28–29 and 138.

"Meek, Carrie P." History, Art & Archives: United States House of Representatives., http://history.house.gov/People/Detail/18110, Accessed Septemenber 19, 2015.

"Meek, Carrie P. 1926–" Encyclopedia.com. Accessed Septemenber 19, 2015, http://www.encyclopedia.com/people/social-sciences-and-law/political-science-biographies/carrie-meek

O'Neill, P. "What Makes a Good Community?" agendaNi. September 2013. https://www.agendani.com/what-makes-a-good-community.

Pittman, Betty J. (granddaughter of Willie and Carry Tanzy Pittman), in discussion with the author, January 8, 2018.

Pittman Jr., Samuel (grandson of Willie and Carry Tanzy Pittman), in discussion with the author, January 19, 2018.

"Polk's Tallahassee City Directory, Yellow Pages and White Pages." 1946–1980. R. L. Polk & Company.

Property Deed 95, Circuit Court, Leon County Court Florida Records, pp. 128–129.

Rabby, G. A. *The Pain and the Promise: The Struggle for Civil Rights in Tallahassee, Florida.* Athens; University of Georgia Press, 1999.

Resolution to Improve Segments of Boulevard Street, City Commission of the City of Tallahassee, Tallahassee, Florida. June 25, 1946.

Resolution to Improve Segments of Canal Street, City Commission of the City of Tallahassee, Tallahassee, Florida. June 25, 1946.

Resolution to Improve Segments of Harrison Street, City Commission of the City of Tallahassee, Tallahassee, Florida. October 13, 1953.

Resolution to Improve Segments of Hudson Street, City Commission of the City of Tallahassee, Tallahassee, Florida. December 13, 1955.

Resolution to Improve Segments of Jennings Street, City Commission of the City of Tallahassee, Tallahassee, Florida. December 13, 1955.

Resolution to Improve Segments of Melvin Street, City Commission of the City of Tallahassee, Tallahassee, Florida. February 9, 1954.

Resolution to Improve Segments of South Bronough Street, City Commission of the City of Tallahassee, Tallahassee, Florida. December 22, 1953.

Resolution to Improve Segments of Van Buren Street, City Commission of the City of Tallahassee, Tallahassee, Florida. June 28, 1955.

Resolution to Improve Segments of Pershing Street, City Commission of the City of Tallahassee, Tallahassee, Florida. December 13, 1955.

"The Ride to Equality: Fifty Years after the Tallahassee Bus Boycott." *Tallahassee Democrat.* May 21, 2006.

"Selected Articles Related to the Civil Rights Movement in Tallahassee, Florida," Florida Memory State Library & Archives. Accessed June 23, 2020.

"Strong Communities." Hertfordshire Community Foundation. March 18, 2016. https://www.hertscf.org.uk/shares/01Aug17151322HCF_StrongCommunities_05_web.pdf

Tacker, H. R. "Household Employment Under OASDHI, 1951–66." Social Security Administration Bulletin. June 1970. https://www.ssa.gov/policy/docs/ssb/v33n6/v33n6p10.pdf

Tallahassee Neighborhood Survey Phase IV. Archaeological Consultants Inc. Volume I. October 1997.

Warranty Deed, Deed Book 21. Circuit Court, Leon County Florida Records. pp. 327–328.

Warranty Deed, Deed Book 36. Leon County Property Appraiser, Leon County Courthouse. p. 446.

Warranty Deed, Record 862. Leon County Property Appraiser, Leon County Courthouse, p. 228.

ACKNOWLEDGMENTS

"Alone we can do so little; together we can do so much."
— Helen Keller

With highest praise to God and the most deeply felt gratitude to all contributors, I present this narrative about the African American neighborhood in Tallahassee, Florida, called Allen Subdivision. Sometimes called Allen or "The Alley," it is the homeplace where I grew up and where I met my beloved extended family—the engine that powered my commitment to complete this work. It was Lavern Washington, leader of current and former Allen residents, who led the charge to document the existence of the community and its contributions to society. My highest respect and gratitude go to Lavern for caring so much and seeing the vision of hard print to describe the splendor of a loving, encouraging, humble, safe, resilient, and spiritually strong African American community whose story demands to be told.

Meeting the charge has required the commitment and stamina to compile, validate, organize, and summarize information needed to appropriately highlight our beloved homeplace. Although the process has been challenging, it also has been incredibly enlightening and rewarding. The process has been made tremendously easier with the help and support of many people, including volunteers and experts. I am deeply grateful for every single person who agreed to complete a survey, tally survey results, grant a telephone or in-person interview, participate in the recording of oral history, helped in developing a composite roster of current or previous Allen residents to be contacted, and who helped in any way to plan for data-gathering events.

I acknowledge and extend a heartfelt thank you to Dr. Jackie Robinson, FAMU Professor of Psychology, and Dr. Bobbie J. Perdue, Professor of Clinical Nursing at Syracuse University, who assisted in reviewing and discussing critical items for the survey instrument used in gathering personal accounts of history from Allen residents. Thank you, Dr. Robinson, for alerting me that the materials gathered and discussed should be published in a book. Your words penetrated and God has spoken! And thank you, Dr. Perdue, for assisting in exploring and clarifying ideas throughout the writing process.

A special thank you goes to Betty Pittman, who took on the arduous task of sending survey session notices to as many Allen residents as possible and hosted a follow-up survey session in her home for individuals who were not able to attend the original survey administration session.

The Allenites who participated in field testing and providing feedback on the draft survey were extremely valuable to this undertaking. From the bottom of my heart, I thank them and all other individuals who actually completed surveys, participated in personal interviews, provided images of and verified facts about their relatives, or who agreed to provide input during video and audio recorded oral history. Equal gratitude is extended to the Allenites who helped to provide transportation for our elders to give their testimonies in recorded sessions.

Indeed, a huge thank you is extended to the internal team of Allenites who helped to tally and check survey results: Queen Bruton, Earline Allison Farmer, Nancy Jefferson Godette, Mary Brewster Hargis, and Cherry Lawrence. The entire tally group and I continue to remember the energizing nourishment provided by our dedicated Allen leader, Lavern Washington, during the long hours required to complete the tallies.

There were three people who literally put the community on the map. They actually helped to create a visual of the geographical Allen neighborhood, as perceived by its long-term residents. A huge thank you goes to Queen Bruton, who got us started with a basic sketch of the Allen area. Based upon the author's research and extensive documentation, Queen's sketch was enhanced to include streets, addresses, and family names for the selected year, 1960. The add-ons were submitted to a graphic artist for professional presentation—Alicia Hope, graphic designer and adjunct instructor at FAMU.

Thank you, Ms. Hope, for creating the official illustration of the community called Allen Subdivision. We are deeply grateful for your patience, understanding, and professional advice on perfecting our starter piece. We also are grateful that you gave your heart, head, hands, and skills to produce the classic and colorful map we can proudly present to the public to illustrate our beloved homeplace. It is of epic proportion, never before (prior to this research) seen in Tallahassee!

Words cannot express the gargantuan debt we owe to Marcus Curtis, GIS Technician II, with the Tallahassee Leon County GIS Department of Development Support and Environmental Management. With a true civic servant spirit, you utilized available city and county electronic files to uncover more facts about our neighborhood based upon the illustration provided by our graphic artist.

Thank you, Mr. Curtis, for confirming the total acreage and verifying the legal boundaries of Allen Subdivision based upon the city and county data made available to you. You went further to produce historic areal maps and a high-quality, colorful display of the initial, connected tracts of land (with the original owners we were able to identify in our research) for the composite neighborhood we call home. We are extremely grateful that you sat with us for hours, sometimes after work, perfecting a graphic of our adored community. It is a tremendously invaluable product!

The work of other supporters who are external to the Allen group also must be acknowledged. Thank you, Heather Whitmore, urban planner of the City of Tallahassee Land Use and Environmental Services Department, for examining photos of selected houses in Allen. You volunteered your time and expertise to provide a technical description of the original homes built in the neighborhood. We sincerely thank you for illuminating a piece of our history that was previously unknown to us. You enriched our knowledge significantly!

Matt Lutz, director of Records Management for the City of Tallahassee Treasurer-Clerk's Office, I am grateful that you provided priceless information regarding the upgrade of homes and streets in the community. Thank you for the time you spent researching city commission resolutions and official newspaper announcements to give our readers an idea of the time period during which permits were issued for changes and upgrades in homes and on the streets in the Allen neighborhood.

Thanks to Dr. Murell Dawson, former director of the FAMU Meek/Eaton Black Archives, Research Center and Museum, for supporting this project. You graciously provided space and staff for the recording of oral testimonies from the highly esteemed elders of the Allen community. In addition, at the museum, you hosted a tour, followed by our Sunday Afternoon Chat and lunch with our elders. The space and the audio and video team you provided richly enhanced our body of knowledge, as shared at the museum by our Super Significant Seniors.

I am deeply grateful also to Mrs. Altamese Barnes, whom I consider to be the leader of extensive documentation and promotion of African American history in Tallahassee communities. Thank you Mrs. Barnes, for meeting with me and giving me reassurance that the preliminary Allen Subdivision narrative included key elements and was appropriate for a story that needed to be told. You also advised me on ways to enhance the story. And, through the Blueprint FAMU Way project, you provided photos that I had not initially attained. I am also grateful for your referring me to other valuable resources for completion of this project.

Dr. Reginald Ellis, FAMU history professor, your contribution was very helpful. Your assignment of a graduate student, My'Eisha Penn, to conduct personal interviews and transcribe responses immensely enhanced this project. Thank you, Dr. Ellis and Ms. Penn!

To Dr. Barbara Cotton, former associate dean of the College of Arts and Sciences and former professor of history at FAMU, words cannot express my gratitude for your willingness to give this document a final, critical eye. Your suggestions were well received and clearly refined the initially written work. Thank you so much!

A word of thanks to City Commissioner Dianne Williams-Cox is also in order. I am deeply grateful for the foreword you provided for this document. My gratitude is extended also for your astute leadership in the city, your support of this work, and your encouragement to verify the details of yet another African American community that has contributed to the rich tapestry of our fair city.

I cannot thank Isabella Folmar enough for her diligence in helping to document details about the Black-owned businesses of Allen. As a collection and outreach librarian with the State Library of Florida, you gave countless hours, far more than I had ever imagined, to help fill in many blanks about the African American-owned venues that once existed in Allen.

To Earl Washington, Allen photographer, Thank you for capturing many of the Allen moments that added life to this narrative. Your work significantly enhanced this project!

To Dr. Aron Myers, director of the Riley House Museum, I am deeply grateful for suggestions and reference materials you provided toward getting this work published. Thank you, too, for your encouragement and help in preparing copy-ready photos in the appropriate resolution needed for this undertaking. Your patience and understanding were incredibly enabling!

My heartfelt gratitude goes out also to Tatiana Daguillard, Blueprint Intergovernmental Agency planner, for being one of the strongest cheerleaders and for being excited about this work. From the bottom of my heart, I thank you also for the use of your sharp and highly valued technological skills in helping to prepare this document for print.

I must acknowledge my dear friends whose encouraging words kept me moving to the completion of this product. From the depths of my heart, I thank Beverly Berry Baker, Dr. Bobbie Perdue, Mrs. Joann Clark, Dr. Jackie Robinson, Dr. Brenda Jarmon, Mrs. Alberta Wilson, Dr. Margaret Timmons, Dr. Freddie Groomes-McLendon, Mrs. Barbara Kelly, Dr. Jerrlyne Jackson and Mrs. Evelyn English. You have all kept me uplifted with your encouraging words, your faith in me, and your embracing this work as important to our local and national communities.

My friend and high school classmate, Dr. Delores Brooks Lawson, is one with whom I have commonly witnessed childhood experiences in Allen and one who has been aware of this work from its beginning. I am eternally grateful for your comments about the value of this work and your continuing words of encouragement. To Leon County Commissioner, William Proctor, Jr., another fellow Baby Rattler, I appreciate your supporting statements and your enthusiasm, too.

To my beloved daughter, Kyra Massey Kennedy, I thank you for your love, support, and encouragement. Throughout my journey, you kept me inspired by your extraordinary accomplishments in the face of your ongoing responsibilities as wife, mother, grandmother, multiple-business owner, inventor, and master's and doctoral student. In the wake of all your personal projects and obligations, you inspired me even further by writing an e-book to help others in their quest to launch nonprofit businesses. You are a phenomenal woman to whom I am eternally grateful and of whom I am exceedingly proud!

Last, but certainly not least, I must express my gratitude to my other family members, including my sisters, Mary Brewster Hargis and Lanell Mills McCaskill; my brother and sister-in-law, Napoleon and Shirlene Mills; my nieces and nephews; my Godsister, Cherry Lawrence and my Goddaughter, Quanitra Thurston. Thank you, Cherry, for being my greatest personal cheerleader indeed from start to finish. To all my family, I am sincerely grateful for your support, your prayers, and enthusiasm about this project. I am also grateful and humbled by your understanding of the importance of this work to our biological family and to our extended Allen Subdivision family.

ABOUT THE AUTHOR

Deloris Mills Massey Harpool is a native of Tallahassee, Florida. She was raised with six siblings on Hudson Street in the south-central Tallahassee neighborhood called Allen Subdivision. She earned a bachelor's degree in sociology and a master's degree in counseling at Florida A&M University (FAMU). She attained the designation of Certified Public Manager (CPM) at Rutgers University of New Jersey.

In thirty-eight years of professional service, Harpool provided leadership in educational access and equal-opportunity programs for students and for executive and administrative personnel in colleges and universities throughout Florida and New Jersey. In the same genre, she served as a consultant in the Republic of South Africa with the US Agency for International Development (USAID). She is a Life Member of Alpha Kappa Alpha Sorority Inc. who attained "Golden" status in 2018 after over fifty years of membership and service.

After retiring as a higher education policy and program director, Harpool became aware of and concerned about notable physical changes in the beloved homeplace where she grew up. Due to urban redevelopment and imminent domain, the number of businesses and families in this humble but once-vibrant African American neighborhood was sadly declining. Yet, beginning in the early 1900s, in spite of segregation, discrimination, disparities in economic opportunities, and other Jim Crow practices, this little-known community thrived and produced African Americans and descendants of remarkable success.

In May of 1971, Deloris was married to the late Edward E. Massey. They had one daughter, Kyra Massey, who with her husband, Warren, later blessed the author with five grandchildren: Nia, Kyren, Roman, London and Kylun Kennedy. One great grandchild, Nyla, was an added blessing. While employed as a program director at Florida A&M University, and in her second marriage, the author became Deloris Massey Harpool.

As in her experience as a young Allenite, Harpool promoted God-centered philosophy, high academic achievement, and perseverance with her daughter and each subsequent generation in her family as the way to purpose, success and upward mobility in life. The profile of her offspring is a working example of the many progenies who were influenced by their parents' achievement motivation and ties to Allen Subdivision. Harpool's daughter, Kyra, received a BS degree in Mathematics, with a minor in Mechanical Engineering. She later became an inventor whose products and intellectual property are registered with the US Office of Patents and Trademarks. In 2021, Kyra earned the MBA degree in Marketing and she is currently pursuing a doctoral degree in organizational leadership via North Central University of Scottsdale, Arizona.

Harpool acknowledges that other success stories for Allen residents and their descendants deserve to be shared. When Tallahassee's redevelopment efforts began to unfold and information was scarce, it became evident that no deep-dive review of the cherished Allen Subdivision and its consequential impact had ever been published. Its legacy and its effect on its sons and daughters and their descendants begged action. To memorialize and preserve its rich history, Harpool saw the urgency and accepted the community's challenge to document the unique character and some of the consequential effects of this treasured place.

This book is the first of its magnitude that Harpool has authored. While her research was well underway in 2015, she contributed to a report produced by FAMU history professors that included key facts about Allen Subdivision. Their report also described other communities connected along Tallahassee's FAMU Way. In addition to research results for three other Allen Subdivision historical markers, Harpool produced content to be displayed in the local Blueprint Intergovernmental Agency's History and Culture Trail Project. She offers these works with hopes that they will enlighten, entertain, uplift, and inspire youth and all readers to explore these and other African American–community success stories.

Printed in the United States
by Baker & Taylor Publisher Services